**Classical Liberalism – A Primer**

T0097286

# CLASSICAL LIBERALISM – A PRIMER

EAMONN BUTLER

Institute of
**Economic** Affairs

First published in Great Britain in 2015 by
The Institute of Economic Affairs
2 Lord North Street
Westminster
London SW1P 3LB
in association with London Publishing Partnership Ltd
www.londonpublishingpartnership.co.uk

The mission of the Institute of Economic Affairs is to improve understanding
of the fundamental institutions of a free society by analysing and expounding
the role of markets in solving economic and social problems.

Copyright © The Institute of Economic Affairs 2015

The moral right of the author has been asserted.

A CIP catalogue record for this book is available from the British Library.

ISBN 978-0-255-36707-3

Many IEA publications are translated into languages other
than English or are reprinted. Permission to translate or to reprint
should be sought from the Director General at the address above.

Typeset in Kepler by T&T Productions Ltd
www.tandtproductions.com

Printed and bound in Great Britain by Page Bros

To my friend John Blundell (1952–2014)

# CONTENTS

# THE AUTHOR

Eamonn Butler is director of the Adam Smith Institute, a leading policy think tank. He has degrees in economics and psychology, a PhD in philosophy, and an honorary Doctor of Letters. In the 1970s he worked in Washington for the US House of Representatives, and taught philosophy at Hillsdale College, Michigan, before returning to the UK to help found the Adam Smith Institute. He is a former winner of the UK's National Free Enterprise Award.

Eamonn is author of books on the pioneering economists Milton Friedman, F. A. Hayek and Ludwig von Mises, a primer on the Austrian School of Economics and *The Condensed Wealth of Nations*. For the IEA, he has written primers on Adam Smith, Ludwig von Mises and public choice theory; his *Foundations of a Free Society* won the Fisher Prize in 2014. He is co-author of a history of wage and price controls, and of a series of books on IQ. His recent popular publications, *The Best Book on the Market*, *The Rotten State of Britain* and *The Alternative Manifesto*, attracted considerable attention, and he is a frequent contributor to print and broadcast media.

## ACKNOWLEDGEMENTS

Once again, I thank Madsen Pirie for his early advice and input, and my other colleagues at the Adam Smith Institute for their forbearance.

## FOREWORD

Classical liberalism is one of the most important of modern political and social philosophies. Indeed, we may say that it was the efforts of believers in this set of ideas that were crucial in bringing the modern world into existence. Without the campaigns, arguments, thinking and analysis of people who defined themselves as classical liberals, many of the essential features of modernity, such as sustained intensive growth, the privatisation of religious identity and the abolition of slavery would not have come about.

Despite its importance, classical liberalism is today poorly understood, often misrepresented (wilfully so in many cases) and wrongly identified with other ways of thinking, notably conservatism. A particular difficulty is the way the American use of the term liberal to mean 'social democrat' means that in the English-speaking world believers in traditional liberalism have had to find a new label for their ideas. (This is not the case in continental Europe, where 'liberal' retains its traditional meaning.) Libertarian has become the widely adopted term but for various reasons this is unsatisfactory.

Given this, Eamonn Butler's account is particularly welcome. It is a wonderfully clear and well set out introduction to what classical liberalism is as a system of thought, whence it came, what it is like now and where it might be going. One valuable feature of the book is the way that it brings out the differences and variety within what nevertheless remains a coherent approach to political thinking and questions of public policy. (The same could be said for socialism and conservatism of course.) It is worth thinking about some of the questions it raises and the ways these might be further explored.

As the historical account indicates, classical liberalism clearly has roots and origins as a political movement in episodes of English history and a way of thinking about law and government that we can trace back to at least the seventeenth century, if not even earlier to Magna Carta and medieval constitutionalism. However, as it makes clear, there is also a source in the history of continental Europe, not least in France (despite F. A. Hayek describing that country as 'the most hopeless for classic liberalism'). This goes back to the Enlightenment and thinkers such as Kant but can also be traced further back, to Renaissance and late-medieval thinkers such as those associated with the School of Salamanca, and to the medieval traditions of constitutional government and limits on royal power, from the Iberian Peninsula to Scandinavia and Poland–Lithuania. Classical liberalism's origins in Europe do not, however, make it a European way of thinking. It should not be seen as a 'Western' ideology; rather it is a perspective that is universal in its orientation and can draw upon compatible and sympathetic traditions in all the world's cultures and civilisations.

In addition to the crucial ideas that this book ably sets out and clearly explains, classical liberalism is also associated with a number of attitudes and qualities of style. One of the most important is that of optimism, of confidence that the human condition can be improved and in the last two centuries has improved. Another related one is that of being forward looking, of looking to the future rather than at the past. We might also identify a focus on individuality and self-governance or autonomy. Perhaps the most important is that of civility and of thinking the best of one's opponents and interlocutors rather than ascribing malevolent purposes and designs to them – a quality lacking in much contemporary discourse.

This work does an excellent job of describing simply and clearly what classical liberalism is, and also of describing by inference what it is not. Clearly, it is distinct from socialism and other forms of egalitarian collectivism such as social democracy and social or 'new' liberalism. It is also not the same as conservatism, being generally more optimistic, more trusting in reason (as opposed to faith or tradition), and less respectful of inherited or traditional institutions. One of the things that becomes apparent on reading this book and which would become even more so on reading much of the suggested further reading, is that far from being conservative, classical liberalism is a radical creed that has already brought about an enormous and profound change in the conditions and ways of life of most of the people in the world, sweeping aside much of the old order in doing this (a point made forcefully by Ludwig von Mises for example). One example of this is the historical association between classical liberalism and feminism, with most of the 'first wave' feminists ardent classical liberals and with many examples of that position to be found today.

Classical liberals as a movement and classical liberalism as a body of ideas have changed much and improved much, but there has also been remission, as the book points out, and there is still much to do. When classical liberals forget this and become rather defenders of the way things are they lose their impetus and a crucial part of their identity. As the work also makes clear with its discussion of new intellectual developments within the tradition, this is not a fixed and perfected body of ideas with sacred texts and everlasting conclusions that require only glossing and commentary. Rather it is a vibrant and living intellectual movement in which the basic insights described here are constantly reapplied and rethought, with new ideas, analyses and proposals being articulated and the hydra's heads of error being assaulted.

At the IEA we do not explicitly endorse a particular political philosophy, much less the position of a specific political party or movement. Nevertheless, the continuing objective of understanding social problems and effectively addressing them rules out certain approaches while being open to others. Classical liberalism is one of the congenial philosophies and movements that arrives at a way of thinking and understanding of the world that is compatible and consonant with this, although it is not the only one.

As such, this book is a welcome addition to the IEA's list and will make a major contribution to better understanding of one of the formative philosophies of the modern age.

STEPHEN DAVIES
*Education Director*
*Institute of Economic Affairs*
May 2015

The views expressed in this monograph are, as in all IEA publications, those of the author and not those of the Institute (which has no corporate view), its managing trustees, Academic Advisory Council members or senior staff. With some exceptions, such as with the publication of lectures, all IEA monographs are blind peer-reviewed by at least two academics or researchers who are experts in the field.

## SUMMARY

- Classical liberals give priority to individual freedom in social, political and economic life. They recognise that different people's freedoms may conflict, and disagree on where the limits to freedom lie, but broadly agree that individual freedom should be maximised and the use of force should be minimised.
- They see the individual as more important than the collective and call for limited, representative government that draws its legitimacy from the people. Governments should themselves be bound by the rule of law, and justice should be dispensed according to accepted principles and processes.
- Classical liberals disagree about the exact role of the state, but generally wish to limit the use of force, whether by individuals or governments. They call for states that are small and kept in bounds by known rules. The main problem of politics is not how to choose leaders, but how to restrain them once they have power.
- Classical liberalism is not the same as American liberalism, which values social freedom but gives much economic power to the state. Nor is it an atomistic idea: it sees individuals as members of various overlapping groups, with many family, moral,

religious or other allegiances. Such civil society institutions are a useful bulwark against central state power.

- Free speech and mutual toleration are viewed as essential foundations for peaceful cooperation between free people. Classical liberals argue that such cooperation gives rise to spontaneous social orders (such as markets, customs, culture and language) that are infinitely more complex, efficient and adaptive than anything that could be designed centrally.
- In economics, classical liberals believe that wealth is not created by governments, but by the mutual cooperation of free individuals. Prosperity comes through free individuals inventing, creating, saving, investing and, ultimately, exchanging goods and services voluntarily, for mutual gain – the spontaneous order of the free-market economy.
- Classical liberalism can be traced back to Anglo-Saxon England and beyond, but derives largely from the ideas of thinkers such as John Locke (1632–1704), Adam Smith (1723–90) and the Founding Fathers of the United States. In recent times, it has been refreshed by scholars such as F. A. Hayek (1899–1992) and Milton Friedman (1912–2006).
- Different classical liberals advance different arguments for freedom. Some see it as a good in itself, others appeal to the idea of natural rights enjoyed by all individuals. Some say that authority over others stems solely from their agreement to submit to laws, embodied in a social contract. A number argue that

social and political freedom simply makes everyone better off.

- Classical liberals also advance different arguments for toleration. Many believe that forcing people to do things against their will is costly and damaging and produces perverse results. Others see no justification for interfering in people's lifestyle choices, provided that nobody else is harmed by them. Some cite the benefits of allowing diverse ideas and opinions.

- Classical liberalism is not a fixed ideology, but a spectrum of views on social, economic and political issues, grounded in a belief in freedom and an aversion to the coercion of one individual by another. It has enjoyed a revival in recent decades, but now faces new and urgent questions – such as the freedom that should be extended to groups who wish to destroy freedom.

# 1   INTRODUCTION

## The purpose of this book

This primer aims to provide a straightforward introduction to the principles, personalities and key developments in classical liberalism. It is designed for students and lay readers who may understand the general concepts of social, political and economic freedom, but who would like a systematic presentation of its essential elements.

The book takes classical liberalism to embrace a wide spectrum of views, all of which consider individual freedom and the minimisation of violence as their top priorities, but which may range from something near libertarianism at one end to more conservative views at the other. It sees classical liberals as believing firmly in individual freedom, but believing that at least some administration of government and justice is needed to maintain it. The debate, among classical liberals at different points on the spectrum, is how large and wide that government role should be.

## Outline of the book

Chapter 2 outlines the ten core principles that unite classical liberals, whatever the differences between them.

Chapter 3 then sets out the historical development of classical liberalism, from its Anglo-Saxon roots, through the Reformation, the Enlightenment and revolutions, to its nineteenth-century decline and its modern revival today.

Chapter 4 considers the arguments for freedom, outlining the different and often conflicting views of classical liberals from different traditions. Chapter 5 then looks at classical liberals' ideas on morality, and the centrality to them of minimising coercion, either from individuals or the state. Chapter 6 outlines the thorny debate on what the role and limits of that state should be. Chapter 7 explains why classical liberals believe that human societies are largely self-regulating and create public benefit without needing any large central authority to maintain them. Chapter 8 shows that this is also true in economics, thanks to the evolution of natural institutions such as markets and prices.

Chapter 9 outlines the recent revival in classical liberal thinking, and some of the new schools of thought that have come up within the classical liberal tradition.

The book concludes with sketches of the contributions of key classical liberal thinkers, some important quotations on classical liberal issues, a timeline of the development of classical liberalism, and further reading.

# 2   WHAT IS CLASSICAL LIBERALISM?

What most defines classical liberals is the priority they give to *individual freedom*. Human beings also have other values, of course – honesty, loyalty, security, family and more. But when it comes to our *social, political* and *economic* life, classical liberals believe that we should aim to maximise the freedom that individuals enjoy.

Classical liberals maintain that people should be allowed to live their lives as they choose, with only the minimum necessary restraint from other individuals or authorities. They accept that freedom can never be absolute, since one person's freedom may conflict with another's: we may all have freedom of movement, but we still cannot all move onto the same spot at the same time. And freedom does not mean you are free to rob, threaten, coerce, attack or murder others, which would violate *their* freedom.

So what are the limits to individual freedom? Classical liberalism has no single answer. It is not a dogmatic set of rules. Classical liberals do not completely agree on where the limits to personal (and government) action should lie. But they do broadly agree that any answer should seek to maximise individual freedom, and that anyone who wants to curb it must have a very good reason.

## Ten principles of classical liberalism

To understand better what classical liberalism is, we can list ten principles that classical liberals all agree on.

### 1. The presumption of freedom

Classical liberals have a *presumption in favour of individual freedom* or liberty (the words are interchangeable in English). They want to maximise freedom in our political, social and economic life. However, they have different grounds for this conclusion.

To many, freedom is *good in itself.* They argue from psychology that, given a choice, people invariably prefer being free to being coerced. Others, natural rights advocates, say that freedom is something given to us by God or Nature. Some argue that freedom is based on a *social contract* that people in a 'state of nature' would have to agree if they were to avoid chaos and conflict.

Many suggest that freedom is an *essential requirement for progress*. Some make a *humanist* point, that freedom is an essential part of what it means to be human: someone who is controlled by others is not a whole person, but a mere cipher. Lastly, *utilitarian* classical liberals value freedom as the best way to maximise the welfare of society as a whole.

### 2. The primacy of the individual

Classical liberals see the individual as more important than the collective. They would not sacrifice an individual's freedom for some collective benefit – at least, not without some very good justification. They have several different reasons for this.

One view – called *methodological individualism* – is that a collective has no existence beyond the individuals that comprise it. Certainly, society is more than a collection of individuals, just as a house is more than a collection of bricks. But *society* has no independent mind of its own; it is *individuals* who think and value and choose and drive events. There is no collective 'public interest' beyond the interests of the individuals who comprise that community.

And, secondly, those individuals disagree. What is in the interest of one person may be against the interest of others. The reality of sacrificing individual freedom to 'the collective' is that we would be sacrificing it to some particular set of interests, not to everyone's interests.

Another reason is simple experience. History explodes with examples of the horrors visited on populations when their freedom is sacrificed to some leader's misconceived notion of the collective good. Even in recent times, one need only reflect on the atrocities of Hitler, the starvation and purges under Stalin, or the mass murders ordered by Pol Pot.

Fourthly, society is hugely complicated and in constant flux. No single authority could possibly know what is best for everyone in this complex, dynamic world. Individuals are far better placed to make decisions for themselves, and should be left free to do so.

## 3. Minimising coercion

Classical liberals want to minimise coercion. They want a world in which people get along by peaceful agreement, not one in which anyone uses force or threats to exploit or impose their will on others.

Accordingly, classical liberals give the monopoly on the use of force to the government and judicial authorities. But they want to keep even that to its necessary minimum; they know how easily power can be abused.

Classical liberals maintain that any use of force to curb people's actions must be *justified*. The onus is on anyone who wants to restrict freedom to show why that is both necessary and sufficiently beneficial to warrant it.

And more generally, classical liberals hold that individuals should be able to live their lives as they choose, without having to ask anyone's permission before they do something. There may be a good reason to curb their actions; but it is up to those who want to do so to make the case.

## 4. Toleration

Classical liberals believe that the main – or perhaps the only – good reason to interfere with people's freedom is to prevent them doing or threatening actual harm to others. They do not believe that we should restrict people's actions just because we disapprove of them or find them offensive.

For example, classical liberals defend free speech, even if some people use this freedom to say things that others – or even everyone else – may think obnoxious. Likewise, individuals should be free to assemble in groups such as clubs, unions or political parties, even if other people find their aims and activities repugnant. They should be free to trade goods and services, even ones (such as drugs and prostitution) of which others might disapprove. And they should have the freedom to live, to hold whatever opinions they please, and practise whatever religion they want.

Classical liberals see such toleration as not just good in itself. They see toleration and mutual respect as essential foundations for peaceful cooperation and the creation of a beneficial, well-functioning society. Human differences are a fact of our social life, and always have been. Liberals do not believe that those differences can be eliminated, and are deeply sceptical of Utopian attempts to do so. Given that, toleration will always be a necessary part of functioning social life.

## 5. Limited and representative government

Classical liberals concede that some force may be needed to prevent people injuring others, and agree that only the authorities should have this power. Yet they know that power is not wielded by some dispassionate 'state' but by actual human beings who have the same failings as the rest of us. They know that power tends to corrupt, and that politicians often cite the 'public interest' for policies that are actually in their own interests.

In addition, social contract theorists such as the English philosopher John Locke (1632–1704) argue that government power comes from individuals, not the other way round. People give up some of their freedoms to the government in order to maximise their freedom in general. So government has no legitimate powers beyond the powers that individuals have themselves; and the whole purpose of government is to expand freedom, not to restrict it. As the American revolutionary thinker Thomas Paine (1737–1809) argued, citizens would be within their rights to overthrow any government that broke this trust.

But revolution is a last resort. Classical liberals believe that *representative and constitutional democracy* is the best means yet discovered for keeping our legislators accountable to the people. Elections are not so much about choosing good leaders, but removing bad ones. The better informed and more vigilant the electorate, the better they work. Even so, democracy has its limits: it may be a good way to make some decisions, but these are few; usually we are better to let individuals make their own choices.

## 6. The rule of law

Another principle that restrains power and creates greater security for the public is the *rule of law*. This is the idea that we should be governed by known laws, not the arbitrary decisions of government officials – what the American statesman John Adams (1785–1836) called 'a government of laws, and not of men'.

Classical liberals insist that the law should apply equally to everyone, regardless of gender, race, religion, language, family or any other irrelevant characteristics. It should apply to government officers just as much as to ordinary people; nobody should be 'above the law'.

To maintain the rule of law requires a system of justice, with independent courts that cannot be manipulated by individuals or governments. There need to be basic judicial principles such as habeas corpus, trial by jury and due process to prevent those in power using the law in their own interests.

The rule of law has another happy consequence – it makes life far more predictable, because it enables us to anticipate how people (including officials) will – and will not – behave. So we can make long-term plans without fear of having them shattered by the caprice of others.

## 7. Spontaneous order

You may think that a large and complex society needs a large and powerful government to run it; but classical liberals dispute this. They believe that government is not the basis of social order. The complex social institutions that we see around us are largely unplanned. They are the result of *human action, but not of human design.*

For example, no central authority or conscious planning was needed to produce language, or our customs and culture, or markets for goods and services. Such institutions simply grow and evolve out of the countless interactions between free people. If, over the centuries, they prove useful and beneficial, they persist; if not, they change or are abandoned.

The Austrian social theorist F. A. Hayek (1899–1992) called the result *spontaneous order.* Spontaneous orders can be hugely complex. They evolve through individuals following rules of conduct – like the rules of grammar – that they might not even realise they are following, and could scarcely describe. It is the height of folly, in politicians and officials, to presume that any single mind could comprehend such complex orders, never mind improve on them.

## 8. Property, trade and markets

Classical liberals believe that wealth is not created by governments, but by the mutual cooperation of individuals in the spontaneous order of the marketplace. Prosperity comes through free individuals inventing, creating, saving, investing and, ultimately, exchanging goods and services voluntarily, for mutual gain – the spontaneous order of the *free-market economy.*

This wealth-creating social order grows out of a simple rule: respect for private property and contract, which allows specialisation and trade.

Freedom and property are intimately related. The market economy, and the wealth it generates, depends on the free movement of people, goods, services, capital and ideas. And the existence of private wealth makes it easier for people to resist the exploitation of a predatory government.

Classical liberals do not allow property to be acquired by force. In fact, most property is *created* – crops are raised, houses are built, innovations are developed. Property clearly benefits the owner. But, in fact, it benefits everyone because it promotes wider prosperity.

## 9. Civil society

Classical liberals believe that voluntary associations are better at providing individuals' needs than are governments. While they emphasise the priority of individuals, they recognise that people are not isolated, *atomistic,* self-centred beings. On the contrary, they are social animals and live in families and groups and communities that partly shape their values – clubs, associations, unions, religions, schools, online communities, campaigns, self-help groups, charities and all the other institutions that we call *civil society*.

These institutions are an important part of how people relate to each other. Our outlook, values and actions are shaped within them. And they provide the basis of mutual understanding on which cooperation can be built. Indeed, cooperation would be impossible without the freedom to associate like this.

Civil society also provides a *buffer* between individuals and governments. If we really were all isolated individuals, our freedoms would be easily suppressed by a despotic government. But the complex intersecting circles of civil society not only demonstrate that alternatives to government action are possible – private charities, for example, instead of state welfare – but also give us the common interest and strength with which to resist.

## *10. Common human values*

Classical liberals, then, wish to harness our common humanity for mutual benefit. They uphold the basic principles of life, liberty and property under the law. Those, they believe, are the foundations of a thriving, spontaneous social order based on mutual respect, toleration, non-aggression, cooperation and voluntary exchange between free people.

Politically, they favour free speech, free association, the rule of law and – since rulers are no more saintly than the rest of us – limits on government that prevent those in authority doing too much harm.

They know that a good society cannot rest solely on human benevolence. It rests more on the peaceful co-operation of different, self-interested individuals. So they favour freedom and equality under the law, with a strong, trustworthy justice system that prevents us harming others, but does not try to direct our lives.

Economically, classical liberals favour freedom in production and exchange, and the free movement of people, goods and capital. They defend private property and wish to keep taxation to what is necessary to provide the public with defence and any other 'public goods' that are under-provided by the market.

This is far from the common caricature of classical liberalism as a tiny, laissez-faire, night-watchman state. Justice alone, for example, is a hugely complex institution that needs great and continuing effort to maintain. Classical liberals know that the protection of life, liberty and property are no small tasks.

---

**Box 1    A note on American liberalism**

---

When Americans speak of 'liberalism', they are talking about something very different from classical liberalism. Classical liberalism, also known as 'old liberalism' or 'liberalism in the European sense' focuses on the freedom of individuals; the minimisation of coercion; property and free exchange; and a limited, accountable government that protects and expands freedom.

American or 'new liberalism' or 'modern liberalism' shares a strong belief in personal freedom, but considers that freedom is more than merely the absence of coercion – it can be fostered by paternalist and interventionist government.

American liberals say that the state has a duty to protect people from themselves and from the unjust inequalities of power that it believes are often created by property ownership. They call for a generous welfare system to compensate the poor and support for workers against their (more powerful) employers. They are sceptical that economic freedom produces public benefits (such as high employment) and believe that the state should intervene in order to expand opportunities, provide public goods and make markets serve the public interest.

Classical liberals are very suspicious of such policies. They fear that government power easily grows far beyond its usefulness; and point out that even the best-intentioned policies often have dismal and unintended consequences.

# 3 CLASSICAL LIBERALISM: THE FAMILY TREE

## Early ancestors

Some classical liberals trace their ideas back to the Chinese philosopher Lao-Tzu, who advocated restraint in leadership. Twenty centuries ago, the Indian emperor Ashoka was also calling for freedom and political tolerance. And Islam embraced economic freedom from its earliest origins in the sixth century.

But these are distant cousins of modern classical liberalism. The direct line is European, indeed specifically English. According to the classical liberal thinker and politician Daniel Hannan (1971–), it starts with the Anglo-Saxons, who from around the year 400 started to settle in what we now call England.

### Anglo-Saxon England

As an island nation, hard to invade, England enjoyed greater stability than continental Europe, and there arose a secure system of property tenure and justice. It was not something anyone intended – just the gradual result of independent-minded Anglo-Saxons standing ox-like in their furrows and establishing their rights against interlopers.

Later, the need to co-exist with the Vikings, who started settling from around 800, led to the equally unintended emergence of a common language and common legal arrangements. In the absence of any European-style feudal authority, what came out of this melting pot was the *common law* – the *law of the land* that evolved through the interactions of individuals, rather than the *law of princes* laid down by the powerful.

The common law remains a key foundation of classical liberalism today. It was not monarchical, but determined by the people themselves. It respected private ownership and contract. It recognised liberty under the law. Nobody had to ask permission before acting: anything not specifically prohibited was legal. The law was everyone's business, and law officers were accountable. Even kings were chosen by a council of elders (the Witan), which would demand their loyalty – rather than the reverse.

## Invasion and rebirth

This came to a sudden end in 1066, with the Norman invasion and military occupation. England became ruled by a European elite, whose language and authoritarian ways separated them from the English population. They imposed feudalism, serfdom, social stratification and top-down law-making – the complete opposite of the freedoms and limited government that the Anglo-Saxons had known.

But within a few generations, the Norman landowners identified more and more with the locals; while King John (1166–1216), insulated behind his French courtiers, came to look increasingly detached and despotic, arbitrarily manipulating the law in order to maximise his tax revenues.

The result, in 1215, was the barons forcing the king to sign a great charter – Magna Carta – of rights and privileges.

Most of the charter is about reasserting people's ancient *property rights*, and protecting them from the arbitrary predations of officialdom – the sort of secure rights of tenure that classical liberals deem of crucial importance today.

But a key part of the charter crystallised *ancient freedoms* – of the church, of cities and of the general population – and classical liberal principles such as trial by jury and the due process of law. It even asserted that the king, like everyone else, would be bound by the 'law of the land'. Government, in other words, would be subject to the *rule of law*.

Though John disavowed the charter, he died soon after. His son Henry III came to the throne as a minor, and power subtly shifted from the monarchy to an assembly of barons. Henry reissued the charter, voluntarily, in 1225. But further confrontations with the barons, mostly over taxes for wars, led to another classical liberal initiative in England – the creation of Parliament.

## The rise of classical liberalism

### Cultural and religious revolutions

The English historian Lord Acton (1834–1902) wrote that: 'Liberty is established by the conflict of powers'. In mainland Europe, the authority of the Roman Empire in the

West and of subsequent feudal lords and monarchs had been challenged by the rise of the Christian Church. They did not consciously develop free institutions, but the mutual limitations that they imposed on each other opened up the opportunity for greater personal freedom.

Two other historical events in Europe cemented the importance of individual freedom over state power. A key part of the cultural revolution that was the Renaissance, roughly between the fifteenth and seventeenth centuries, was the introduction of the printing press into Europe in 1450. This simple invention broke the elites' monopoly over science and learning, making knowledge accessible to ordinary individuals. No longer did anyone have to consult authorities for guidance and permission: they had the information on which to base their own choices.

The Protestant Reformation, sparked by Martin Luther in 1517, reinforced this further. It challenged the power of the Catholic Church, and raised the self-esteem of ordinary people by asserting that they could have direct, personal and equal access to God, without needing the intermediation of an elite priesthood.

All this served to raise the position and importance of the individual over the established institutions of power. In the countries where this greater freedom flourished most, art, industry, science and commerce flourished too.

## Political revolution

Politically, things were also changing. A pro-freedom mass movement, the Levellers, swept over England in the

1650s. It was led by John Lilburne (1614–57), who insisted that people's rights were inborn rather than bestowed by government or law. Arrested for printing unlicensed books (in defiance of the official monopoly), he appeared before the notorious Star Chamber, but refused to bow to the judges (insisting that he was their equal) or accept their procedures. Even in the pillory he continued to argue for freedom and equal rights, and inevitably he was imprisoned for his challenge to authority – as he would be several times more.

Lilburne became a popular anti-establishment figure. He petitioned for the end of state monopolies and spelt out what amounts to a bill of rights. This was taken further by Richard Overton (c. 1610–63), also imprisoned for refusing to acknowledge the judicial authority of the House of Lords, who called for a written constitutional 'social contract' between free people whom he saw as having property in their own persons that could not be usurped by anyone else.

## Curbing the power of monarchs

After the English Civil War (1642–51), the reigning monarch, Charles I, was put on trial and executed for high treason – a stark assertion of the limits on government authority.

But the power relationship between king and Parliament had already turned. The island nation of Great Britain (as it had become) needed no standing army to protect itself against frequent invasions. So, unlike continental Europe, the monarch had no force that could be used to repress and exploit the public. Charles needed Parliament to agree to raise taxes for foreign wars.

This frustrated a jealous monarch and led to many conflicts. Among other things, Charles suspended Parliament, sought to levy taxes without its consent and attempted forcibly to arrest five of its most prominent members. He had broken the implicit contract with the people, by which their rights were secured.

## The Glorious Revolution

After an interregnum (1649–60) under the dictatorship of Oliver Cromwell, the balance of authority was made evident again when Charles's son Charles II had to appease Parliament in order to return as king. When his successor, Charles's second son, James II, was deposed, it was Parliament who invited William (the Dutch Prince of Orange) and Mary to the throne. The direction of authority, from people to monarch, could not have been clearer.

In 1689, William and Mary signed the Bill of Rights, an assertion of the rights and liberties of British subjects and a justification of the removal of James II on the grounds of violating those rights and liberties. It called for a justice system independent of monarchs, an end to taxation without Parliament's consent, the right to petition government without fear of retribution, free elections, freedom of speech in Parliament and an end to 'cruel and unusual punishments'. It would directly inspire another great classical liberal initiative, America's own Bill of Rights, a century later.

### John Locke (1632–1704)

John Locke drew together the older tenets of classical liberalism into a recognisably modern body of classical liberal thinking. Part of his purpose was to show how James II had forfeited his throne by violating the social contract. All sovereignty, he asserted, comes from the people, who submit to it solely in order to boost their security and expand their general freedom. When this contract is broken, individuals have every right to rise up against the sovereign.

Locke also developed *natural rights* theory, arguing that human beings have inherent rights that exist prior to government and cannot be sacrificed to it. Governments that infringe these rights were illegitimate.

But central to Locke's ideas was private property, and not just physical property. Locke maintained that people have property in their own lives, bodies and labour – *self-ownership*. From that crucial understanding, he reasoned that people must also have property in all the things that they had spent personal effort in creating – 'mixed their labour' with. The principle of self-ownership therefore makes it crucial that such property should be made secure under the law.

These ideas would inform many of the thinkers behind the American Revolution.

### The Enlightenment

The eighteenth century saw another revival of classical liberal thinking. In France, Montesquieu (1689–1755) developed the idea that in a free society and free economy, individuals have to conduct themselves in ways that maintain peaceful cooperation between them – and do so without needing direction from any authority. He therefore called for a system of checks and balances on government power – another idea that would inform American thinkers.

Meanwhile, a growing intellectual revolt against the authoritarianism of the church led to thinkers such as Voltaire (1694–1778) calling for reason and toleration, religious diversity and humane justice. In economics too, intellectuals such as Turgot (1727–81) argued for lifting trade barriers, simplifying taxes and more competitive labour and agricultural markets.

The Scottish philosopher and economist Adam Smith (1723–90) explained, along the lines of Montesquieu, how, in many cases, the free interaction between individuals tended to produce a generally beneficial outcome – an effect dubbed the *invisible hand*. Self-interest might drive our economic life, but we have to benefit our customers to get any benefit for ourselves.

Smith railed against official monopolies, trade restrictions, high taxes and the suffocating cronyism between government and business. He believed that open, competitive markets would liberate the public, especially the working poor. His ideas greatly influenced policy and ushered in a long period of free trade and economic growth.

## The Rechtsstaat

On the European continent, meanwhile, thinkers such as the German philosopher Immanuel Kant (1724–1804) were developing the principles of the 'just state' or *Rechtsstaat*, which would inform the creation of the American and French constitutions in the late eighteenth century.

Kant argued for a written constitution as a way of guaranteeing permanent peaceful co-existence between diverse individuals, which in turn he saw as a basic condition for human happiness and prosperity. He dismissed the Utopian idea that moral education could curb those differences and make everyone's aims coincide. The state was about enabling diverse individuals to come together for mutual benefit, and the constitution is what held it together.

In the Rechtsstaat, the institutions of civil society – voluntary associations such as clubs, societies and churches – would have an equal role in promoting this social harmony. Government powers would be restrained by the separation of powers, and judges and politicians would be accountable to and bound by the law. The law itself would have to be transparent, explained and proportionate. The use of force would be strictly limited to the justice system. The test of a government is its maintenance of this just constitutional order.

## Success and reassessment

### A new home for classical liberalism

Thomas Paine took many of Locke's classical liberal ideas on natural rights and social contracts, and that government is a necessary evil that can become intolerable if unchecked. In January 1776 he wove them into his influential call to arms, *Common Sense,* indicting Britain as being in breach of its contract to the colonists.

It was natural therefore that, after the hostilities, the Americans should seek a new classical liberal contract between themselves and the government they were creating. The Constitution would be infused with Locke's ideas of natural, inalienable rights, and a Montesquieu-style division of government powers.

## The nineteenth century

But new and radical classical liberal ideas returned to Britain. By 1833, classical liberal activists had secured the abolition of slavery throughout most of the British Empire, and by 1843 the reform was complete.

Also on the social front, the British philosopher and economist John Stuart Mill (1806–73) articulated the 'no harm' principle – that people should be able to act as they please, provided they do not harm others in the process, and thereby diminish their freedom. He also argued for a 'personal sphere' that the state could not touch, and, following the utilitarian philosopher Jeremy Bentham (1746–1832), argued that freedom was the best way to maximise public benefit, or 'utility'.

In economics, the Anti-Corn-Law League, which sought to end protectionist taxes on imported wheat, grew into the Manchester School, whose leading figures such as Richard Cobden (1804–65) and John Bright (1811–89) called for laissez-faire policies on trade, industry and labour.

## *Reappraisal and decline*

However, rapid industrialisation after the mid nineteenth century brought challenges for classical liberalism, such as poor working conditions, social stratification, displacement and urban poverty. Increasingly, people called on governments to regulate away such ills.

Then in the twentieth century, hostilities and threats in Europe promoted a nationalist culture and greater faith in the role of the state. After each wartime expansion, governments failed to shrink back again. In 1913, before World War I, government expenditure was just 17 per cent of GDP in France, 15 per cent in Germany and 13 per cent in the United Kingdom. It is now roughly three times that as a percentage of GDP, and many times more in absolute terms.

Meanwhile, just as the physical scientists were shaping the physical world, so economists and sociologists fancied that they could shape human society scientifically too. They saw central planning as more rational than the natural disorderliness of markets, with their externalities and their supposed tendency to monopoly or to unemployment. No longer was the onus on interventionists; now the classical liberals were the ones who had to justify their demands to let freedom prevail.

# The modern revival of classical liberalism
## *Policy problems and the classical liberal response*

But the vaulting confidence of the interventionists was misplaced. Economies became racked with unemployment and inflation (sometimes, inexplicably for them, at the same time), low growth and crises in housing, energy, lending and foreign exchange markets where governments set prices or manipulated supply and demand. A growing welfare state was plagued by problems of dependence and lack of incentives. There seemed no way to reduce the size of government, nor the demands it was making on taxpayers.

Even though they were on the defensive, classical liberals of many shades had been thinking about such problems for a long time. They went back to the old classical liberal principles and re-thought them, developing new or updated arguments that were better suited for the changed times. Eventually, in the 1980s, this intellectual revolution would inform the policies of world leaders such as Ronald Reagan in the United States and Margaret Thatcher in Britain.

## *Intellectual developments*

The Austrian School economists, starting with Carl Menger (1840–1921), had recognised that economics was not a science but a matter of individual values and actions. Austrians like Ludwig von Mises (1881–1973) and F. A. Hayek (1899–1992) realised that state controls distort economic signals, setting off unpredictable consequences.

In Chicago, meanwhile, Frank Knight (1885–1972) also put individuals at the centre of economics, reasserting that society was a collection of individuals, with no choosing mind of its own. Milton Friedman (1912–2006) argued for government that was strictly limited to creating the conditions (such as monetary stability) within which individuals could build their own social and economic life. Ronald Coase (1910–2013) discovered that markets could solve problems such as pollution, while government intervention may simply worsen matters.

In 1947 Hayek assembled a group of economists, historians and political scientists for a conference to debate some of the key challenges facing classical liberalism in the dark post-war era. The Mont Pelerin Society, as it became known, has since grown to several hundred members, including Nobel laureates and others of influence. It remains a focus for classical liberal ideas and debate.

Another post-war development was the Public Choice School, which came to prominence under James M. Buchanan (1919–2013) and Gordon Tullock (1922–2014) at the University of Virginia. It showed that while mainstream economists spoke of *market failure* and applied cost–benefit analysis to create 'rational' policy in the 'public interest', they forgot about *government failure*. This may manifest itself in imperfections in the political process or the self-interest of those involved in the process.

Elections, for example, are not a test of 'public interest' but a contest of competing interests; a 50%+1 simple majority rule makes it too easy for minorities to be exploited; politicians must appease interest groups to be elected, and lobbyists use this to extract benefits for themselves; and the officials who implement policy have their own interests as well. The conclusion, as classical liberals already knew, is that private decision-making is generally better than political decision-making – which should be limited to where it is strictly necessary in order to protect individual freedoms.

## The diversity of classical liberal ideas

Classical liberals have a range of views about the role of the state, from those who would grant it considerable involvement in the provision of social welfare and public goods, to others, more *libertarian* in outlook, who would restrict it to very little. But small government need not imply a small, mean society.

The American philosopher Robert Nozick (1938–2002), for example, argued for a minimal state, for protection only. Such a state provides a secure framework within which people can create their own mini-Utopias, coming together to form communities, cooperating and deciding which freedoms they might surrender in return for the services of their chosen group. Less libertarian classical liberals would disagree; though they would all celebrate the diversity and dynamism of the society that Nozick envisages.

# 4  CLASSICAL LIBERALISM AND FREEDOM

## The arguments for freedom

There is, then, a wide spectrum of views among classical liberals about the role of the state. Nevertheless, all give priority to freedom in our personal, economic and social lives, and defend everyone's right to life, liberty, property and the pursuit of happiness. Yet they have different reasons for their belief in these principles.

### Freedom as a good in itself

Many see freedom as a good, worth pursuing in itself. When given the chance, most people opt to live their lives in their own way, rather than be dictated to by others. They want self-choice and autonomy. This indicates that people value freedom; so by expanding freedom and reducing coercion, we boost the welfare of individuals, and therefore of the community.

### Natural rights

A strong theme among many classical liberals, from John Locke through the American founding fathers such as

Thomas Jefferson (1743–1826) and still today, is the assertion that individuals have certain *natural rights*. These they see as an inherent part of our humanity which we cannot give up and which do not depend on laws or governments for their existence.

Our natural rights, they say, do not come from laws, customs, religions, beliefs, culture or government, but exist naturally in human beings. They are universal to us all, and inalienable – we cannot sell them, give them away or deny them because they are part of our very humanity.

There are different views on what these core rights actually are, though Locke spoke for many when he listed life, liberty and property: people have a right to live, and to do as they choose provided they do not infringe the equal right of others, and to enjoy all that they create or gain through gifts or trade – but not by force. Being an essential part of us, we cannot give these rights away. We cannot sign ourselves into slavery, because we would be violating our own rights, trying to give up something we cannot give up. Nor can they be legislated away or taken by others.

This idea of natural rights, enjoyed by everyone, challenged the supposedly *divine right* of kings; and the American colonists cited the British government's attempts to suppress their basic rights as justification for their rebellion against it.

This line of thinking elevates freedom above all else. For there to be any rights at all, there must first be liberty, since if we are not free to act, we cannot exercise any of our other rights (other than our freedom of thought, which nobody could prevent). Liberty is the essential condition that allows us to exercise our rights, and the state of affairs in which those rights are respected.

## The social contract

The English political philosopher Thomas Hobbes (1588–1679) argued that any supposed rights and freedoms would be of scant value in a 'state of nature' where brutality was unrestrained; to live peacefully, we would have to accept limits on ourselves and create new *civil rights* and obligations. Though Hobbes is not widely regarded as a classical liberal, Locke followed his social contract method, arguing that in a natural world of free, independent individuals, nobody would have any *entitlement* to rule others; but if people agreed to create and respect a civil authority that could curb violence, they could open up new opportunities and so *expand their freedoms*. More recently, the American philosopher John Rawls (1921–2002), in a similar approach, argued that, given the opportunity of creating a new society and mindful of life's uncertainties, people would opt for a social contract that only tolerated differences between outcomes if those differences worked to the advantage of the worst off.

None of the social contract authors suggested that there ever was some historic moment in which free, independent individuals actually signed some contractual agreement. Their theories are merely 'thought experiments' to explain what rational principles should underpin government.

However, the results always seem to justify their own views. Hobbes's social contract, for example, favours a strong *monarchy* – something that had been shaken by the English Civil War – while the French revolutionary thinker Jean-Jacques Rousseau (1712–78), by contrast, based his social contract on *republican* virtues. For Locke, political authority comes only through the consent of the governed, who therefore have a *right to rebel* if that 'contract' is broken – so justifying the overthrow of James II. Rawls's system, meanwhile, reflects the more *egalitarian* political views of his time.

The American rebellion took heart from Locke's contract theory, and America's Bill of Rights was heavily based on his natural rights view. But social contract theory is not necessarily founded on the existence of natural rights: Hobbes's, for example, is a mere expedient to reduce conflict.

Social contract theory tries to identify the *rational basis* for government. But in reality, life is not so neat. We are social creatures, but we have many conflicting views on what might constitute a good society – no 'rational agreement' seems possible. And when anyone has tried to create a supposedly 'rational' society, the result is always disaster. The French Revolution, based on Rousseau's blueprint, showed Europe the terror that could be visited on the public by such thinking.

## History and progress

A few classical liberals, such as Mill and the contemporary American political scientist Francis Fukuyama (1952–), have seen freedom as part of the march of progress – its economic benefits (allowing individuals to innovate, to work as they choose, to build capital and create wealth) and its civil benefits (justice, security and representative government) being so obvious that it will inevitably be adopted by more and more of humanity. There may be something in this; but we should recall that there are strong tendencies in the opposite direction too.

## Public utility

Still other classical liberals, including the Scottish Enlightenment thinkers Adam Smith and David Hume (1711–76), stress the general public benefits that result from freedom. Freedom, they argue, greatly expands the choices available to individuals, and individuals are far better at making their own judgements about ends and means than some distant authority. So choice boosts the welfare of individuals and, thereby, the welfare of the community as a whole.

These early classical liberals saw no conflict between individual freedom and public welfare 'as if by an invisible hand', as Smith put it, the one creates the other. But they knew that the exact relationship was complex, delicate and imperfect. We could not rely solely on the principle of *love thy neighbour*: self-interest, a far stronger sentiment, needs to be channelled in productive directions. So to avoid harm and maintain harmony required guidance through the rules of ethics, custom and tradition, plus a little coercion through law and the justice system.

To these thinkers, it was freedom that creates public utility, not the other way round. Bentham, by contrast, argued that rights meant nothing unless backed up by the force of law: natural rights were 'nonsense' and inalienable natural rights were 'nonsense upon stilts'. Likewise, the American jurist Oliver Wendell Holmes Jr (1841–1935) argued that rights such as free speech are created by government, and allowed only because they are good for society as a whole.

Many classical liberals recoil at this line of thought. It suggests that government can decide our rights as it pleases; and that our rulers have special rights above ours, namely the right to decide what rights we should have; and that there are no rights except what the majority choose to allow. That, they fear, leaves minorities completely unprotected.

## An expression of individuality

Mill, Smith and Hume make a further point, that freedom allows people to express their personality and diversity. That is beneficial to the community as a whole, opening up specialisation and opportunity. But even more important is the *moral* dimension. People cannot be whole human beings, nor show any judgement, human feeling or moral responsibility, if someone else directs all their actions.

## Methodological individualism

As we have seen, classical liberals see the individual as more important than the collective, since the collective has no life beyond the life of individuals. Human beings may be social creatures, but they *think* and *act* as *individuals*.

People speak of the 'public interest', but in reality there is no mathematical equation by which we can trade off the interests of one person against others. The harm (say, the disappointment, anger or grief) we cause the one and the benefit (such as joy or happiness) we cause others are human emotions that cannot be measured. So we cannot justify sacrificing the freedom of the individual to the supposed but unmeasurable benefit of the group.

It is true that our life as social creatures shapes our views and values. We have social bonds and instincts that impel us to help and comfort others around us, particularly those close to us. And we accept social institutions, customs, habits and moral rules which are generally beneficial to us all, because they enable us to predict with some accuracy how others will behave, allowing us to make better plans and decisions. But these institutions and regularities are the *unintended consequences* of individual actions; it is hugely presumptuous to imagine that we can consciously direct individuals' actions and somehow produce a better overall social result.

## Positive and negative liberty

Classical liberal freedom is essentially *negative*. It is about not being limited by the threats, coercion or interference of others – specifically, *other individuals* or the *institutions*, such as government, that they create. It is *not* about any *physical* limitations – such as our inability to jump ten feet in the air, as the British philosopher Isaiah Berlin (1909–97) put it.

But some thinkers advocate a *positive* approach to freedom. To be truly free, they argue, we must possess the power and resources to exercise our freedom. If you are too poor to afford a Rolls-Royce, you are hardly 'free' to own one. And, even more tellingly, if you are gripped by some addiction, you are not free: to be free, your actions must not only be your own, but must be reflective and considered.

Of course, we all want to reduce *both* human and physical limitations on our freedom of action. That is why we invent medicines that relieve our arthritis and machines that let us fly. But classical liberals are suspicious of the *positive liberty* idea. For a start, as Hayek explained, it mixes up *freedom* with *power*. You are certainly *free* to own a Rolls-Royce – there is no person or law stopping you – but you may not have the purchasing *power* to do so. You are *free* to jump ten feet in the air – nobody will try to stop you – but you may not have enough *power* in your muscles to achieve it.

Classical liberals also worry that the positive liberty approach puts too much trust in the rationality and objectivity of the human authorities. Too often, some government or elite group claims that, like those whose senses are clouded by drugs, we cannot 'really' see what is in our own best interests – and that they have to decide for us. This is patronising to the public, who generally have a much better grasp of their interests than any remote official; it has also been used to justify all sorts of social engineering projects that have ultimately proved disastrous.

## Rights and freedoms

The difference between *rights* and *freedom* is subtle, and perhaps best seen by looking at their opposites. The opposite of *freedom* is *slavery* – being *constrained* by others. The opposite of *right* is *duty* – an *obligation* or claim on others. Hence we speak of *freedom of conscience*, because nobody can prevent you thinking for yourself and because your free thought imposes no obligations on anyone else. But we speak of the *right to life*, because your physical existence imposes a legal or moral *duty* on others to respect it and not to injure or end it. Likewise, you are *free* to acquire property through peaceful trade with others, and you have a *right* to hold and enjoy that property without others stealing it.

Classical liberals like to think that rights exist prior to governments – the laws laid down by government may help to consolidate and preserve them, but no government can override them, however large its majority. As Mill says, we should have the right to speak freely, even if *everyone* disagrees with us: rights are not subject to mere numbers.

However, it is hard to define exactly what these rights should be. Classical liberals are fierce defenders of property rights; but, to take an example from the American economist Milton Friedman (1912–2006), does your ownership of a piece of land prevent me flying an aircraft far above it? (Or today, we might say, a fracking company drilling far below it?) The reality is that these rights have to be refined in public debate and defined in the courts.

Some rights plainly trump others. As Mill explained, your right to swing your fist stops at my nose; while your right of free speech does not extend to endangering other people's safety by falsely shouting 'Fire!' in a crowded theatre. But again, as Hayek asked, does your right of ownership to a well in the desert mean you can deny water to a person dying of thirst – or would that violate their right to life? It seems a matter of opinion: but classical liberals would see a huge danger in having our 'rights' decided by the majority view.

## Restraints on freedom

The central question for classical liberals, therefore, is what, if anything, justifies curbing people's freedom of action – and the further questions of who decides, and how.

It would be so easy if we could measure and sum people's interests, and decide on the basis of what produced the highest value. But human values are personal – or *subjective* – and cannot be summed in this way. We give government the monopoly on coercion precisely so that it can make and enforce such decisions. But we cannot safely leave the process wholly up to state officials because they too have their own subjective interests that inevitably contaminate their decisions.

What classical liberals do agree on is that the burden of proof should fall on those who want to intervene. There should be no use of force to restrict people's freedoms unless that can be justified clearly and rationally. Otherwise, we should leave people to run their own lives. They may be fallible, but even that is better than having our rights and freedoms put at the mercy of distant, ill-informed, self-interested and superficial politicians.

## 5　CLASSICAL LIBERAL MORALITY

## Coercion and toleration

Classical liberals agree that coercion is generally undesirable. Allowing people to impose their will on others through aggression, threats, intimidation or violence does not make for a good society. Regardless of whether it is other individuals or the government using force, if we can avoid it, we should.

However, there will always be conflicts between free people. They will disagree about matters of ownership, and one person's actions may harm another. So in the interests of maintaining peace and curbing violence, we need an impartial system of justice that settles such disputes and discourages aggression. But we cannot rely on everyone to respect those judgements and rules willingly: to keep the peace we will inevitably need to use some of the coercive force that classical liberals dislike so much.

Classical liberals resolve this dilemma by giving the monopoly of force to the state – an institution that they are wary of, but which they hope will be more dispassionate in using force than would ordinary people, left to themselves.

## Harm, not disapproval

So justice requires force; but force requires justification. And to classical liberals, the proper use of this institutional force is very specific: to prevent people harming or threatening others – that is, to minimise the use of violence and coercion in general. But it has to be *real* harm, or the *threat of real harm* to others. Classical liberals are adamant that coercion should *not* be used against individuals simply because we disapprove of them or their actions.

We may well detest other people's religion, reject their political views, abhor their lifestyle, despise their manner and loath their habits. We may be shocked by their ideas and opinions. We may even worry that they are damaging their own health with drugs or their own prospects with their anti-social behaviour. But none of these are valid reasons for using force to try to make them act differently. Classical liberals say that people's beliefs, manner, lifestyle or moral choices are not worthy of prohibition using the drastic coercive power of the state. We are free to try to help them – in overcoming a drug habit, say – but if their actions have no victims apart from themselves, we cannot justify using force.

But classical liberals are sceptical of the argument that people must be 'educated' in order to make 'meaningful' or 'correct' choices. Obviously, people who have better information – such as the potential risks of drugs, or the number of calories in foods – make better-informed choices. But classical liberals hold that most people are better informed than most interventionists imagine. They are certainly better informed about their own aims, opportunities and personal circumstances than any politician ever could be. And however much information they have, their ultimate choices remain a matter of personal judgement, not something that is objectively 'correct' or 'incorrect'. Classical liberals worry that too often the 'education' argument is advanced by interventionists as a way to impose their own values on the choices of other people.

## The arguments for toleration

Classical liberals have many reasons, both moral and practical, for such stress on toleration.

### Cost and harm

First is the enormous *cost* of trying to persuade people to change their deeply cherished beliefs and practices. The cost may be *financial*, such as the vast expense of raising armies, defences and the tax to pay for them during the religious Crusades of the Middle Ages. Or it can be a *human* cost, such as the harassment of the early Christians by the Roman authorities, the persecutions of Protestants during the Reformation, and the killing of Muslims by Serbian Christians in the 1990s.

As the French philosopher Montesquieu (1689–1755) pointed out, there is a far greater chance of peace if religious beliefs are not a matter for politics. And of course political differences have cost humanity dearly too. In just over a century, we have seen the slaughter of two world wars, Stalin's purges in the Soviet Union, Mao's cultural revolution, the mass killings of opponents of the Khmer Rouge, and much more.

Was anything gained by this cost? While people can certainly be terrorised, it remains near impossible to change their deeply held beliefs. And how would we know if we had? In the words of Elizabeth I of England (1533–1603), we cannot 'make windows into men's souls'. Nor should we bother trying, according to Jefferson, since no harm is done by religious differences: 'The legitimate powers of government extend to such acts only as are injurious to others. But it does me no injury for my neighbour to say that there are twenty gods, or no god. It neither picks my pocket nor breaks my leg.'

## Diverse interests

A second classical liberal argument for toleration is that we cannot justify the use of force to alter people's beliefs, lifestyle or morals, when we simply *cannot agree* what is acceptable, unacceptable, tolerable or intolerable. As Kant argued, when people disagree so much on what is tolerable, we really need to be trying to *justify* our views to others, rather than trying merely to *impose* them.

Isaiah Berlin, more recently, explained that individuals each have many different values – such as security, autonomy, family, wealth and comfort – and they each rank them differently too. So it may be perfectly rational of them to choose different ways to live. There is no objective way of deciding whether different people's values are more worthy or less worthy, or whether their rankings are better or worse. It is simply a matter of opinion whether wealth is preferable to comfort, or family is more important than security. In a world where human goals are so diverse, nobody can make choices that are right for everyone.

Instead of trying to impose our views on others, therefore, classical liberals say we must accept that other people are moral beings, who make considered choices that are equally worthy of our respect. We may not always like them but we should respect them, and they in turn should respect the choices we make.

## The benefits of diversity

John Stuart Mill argued that the only justification for interfering with others was to prevent harm or the threat of harm; but differences of opinion do no harm to people who tolerate them. In fact, Mill thought there were many positive reasons why we should actually *welcome* such differences of opinion, rather than trying to censor them. Individuality, originality, innovation and diverse ideas, he thought, fuel the evolution of human progress.

And even if someone expresses an opinion that is plainly wrong in the view of most other people, it might still benefit us. It might, on consideration, turn out to be right, or to contain some element of truth and wisdom that helps advance public understanding. Even if the perspective is completely false, it may still provide a useful challenge to a prevailing opinion that, if taken for granted, would have degenerated into an empty dogma. As Oliver Wendell Holmes observed, the best test of truth is the marketplace of ideas.

## Diversity and moral development

A further argument for toleration is the *moral development* of individuals. The Prussian philosopher and diplomat Wilhelm von Humboldt (1767–1835), for example, argued that the highest purpose of human beings is self-cultivation: so each must have the greatest possible freedom and variety of experiences from which to draw. The state should have only a *night-watchman* role, protecting us against trespass, but not interfering in our self-development.

Mill had a comparable moral view. Interference in other people's actions, he argued, curbs their development as moral human beings. They can never learn and develop from taking responsibility for their choices unless they actually make choices of their own. We cannot respect them as praiseworthy or moral human beings if someone else directs all their actions; they would be more like robots than human beings.

## Perverse results

Another point is that intolerant policies generally *do not work*, or have *unwelcome consequences*, or actually *achieve the opposite* of what their authors intend.

As an example of the first, we have already seen how difficult it can be to shake people's religious beliefs. Similarly, legislative attempts to clamp down on the use of recreational drugs have been ineffective.

A stark example of the second would be the unwelcome consequences of the Prohibition era in the United States (1920–33). Motivated in large part by moral disapproval of alcohol and the saloon culture, Prohibition drove the trade underground, leaving it to those who were willing to break the law. The result was escalating gang violence, corruption among police and public officials, and a widespread disrespect for a law that could not be properly enforced.

Other prohibitions on lifestyle choices, such as prostitution and drugs, have had similar consequences, with the emergence of drug cartels, turf wars and human trafficking. And it has become harder to tackle the real problems created by these activities (such as sexually transmitted infections and addiction), precisely because they have been driven underground, out of reach of the authorities. Ordinarily law-abiding people are turned into criminals, have to deal with criminals, and are put in danger because there is none of the quality control or customer protection that they would get in a legal market. Meanwhile, enforcement resources are diverted from activities that actually do real harm to others.

Third, there are many examples of illiberal policy producing the opposite effects of those intended. For example, attempts to prevent discrimination in the workplace and ensure that merit is properly recognised have led to 'positive discrimination', with people being employed because they fill the quotas, rather than on merit. State education, designed to prevent religious or political groups capturing the minds of young people, has become a monopoly in which there is little or no escape from the prevailing orthodoxy at all. Similarly, religious or political repression has simply stoked up resentments that eventually burst out in violence against the repressors. And at worst, the ideological dogmas of an over-powerful state such as the former Soviet Union can hold up personal, social and scientific progress for decades.

## The slippery slope

When we do use the coercive power of the state to suppress ideas, attitudes and behaviours that we disapprove of, there is no obvious stopping point. Mill warns against the 'tyranny of prevailing opinion', explaining that even if *everyone* thinks that certain views or actions should be suppressed, that is no justification for doing so. There should remain a 'personal sphere' of action and opinion that the state cannot interfere in.

That is only partly because people tend to make better decisions for themselves than distant lawmakers and officials can do – after all, they are more aware of their exact circumstances. Another reason is that it becomes too easy for the majority to presume that they have the *right* to interfere in people's lives, simply because they have numbers on their side. But such easy confidence allows the majority, armed with the instruments of state coercion, far too much latitude to extend their interference and to usurp people's fundamental freedoms.

It is a slippery slope. Interference in one part of people's lives is used to justify parallel interference in others. Often, state intervention will fail or have perverse results, which are then seen as an argument for yet further intervention. The ineffectiveness and unintended consequences of drugs policy, for example, are used as reasons to clamp down even harder, which raises the risks of supplying and using drugs even higher, and makes the resulting problems even worse.

## *Drawing the line*

So where do we draw the line? What are the limits of state intervention? Which activities are tolerable, and which intolerable? What rights should parents have over their own children, for example? Have they the right to smack them, to practice circumcision on them, or even to drink alcohol and take drugs while they are in the womb? Or more generally, should comedians and cartoonists have the free-speech right to mock a religion, if such acts might well provoke violence in which innocent people could be harmed?

There are no clear answers to such questions; different people have different opinions. Narrowing down the answers is the most critical task for classical liberals. They want the coercive power of the state to be focused as precisely as possible, so that it deters and punishes action that is genuinely harmful. Quite where that limit is must be a matter of public discussion and debate: we are unwise to allow our political leaders to decide it for us. But the large mass of action that might cause only minor distress to others should be a matter for argument and persuasion rather than for the iron fist of the state.

## Toleration and the state

The ancient Greeks had no such qualms. Plato (c. 427–347 BC) and Aristotle (384–322 BC), for example, believed that if something is good, the authorities should enforce it. And still today, many people believe that the law should prohibit things that we consider immoral.

Mill accepted that much immoral conduct is potentially damaging, which is precisely why we consider it immoral. But other acts that might be called immoral may cause no harm to others: the supposed victim might even regard it as beneficial, as with assisted suicide, for example. Using the coercive power of the state against such benign conduct would only reduce human welfare.

All classical liberals are sceptical of state power, and those at the more libertarian end of the spectrum believe the state is more likely to damage our freedom than to promote it. Hence Mill's no-harm rule: if we start banning things that neither cause nor threaten demonstrable harm, we could end up banning everything. For Locke or Jefferson, the state existed solely to protect citizens and expand their freedoms: dictating someone's lifestyle, or promoting a particular religion or ethical code, was no part of its business. That is why America's First Amendment insists on not merely religious toleration, but religious freedom.

## Risk and the use of force

But interventionists argue that every action has at least some potentially harmful consequences for other people, so each case must be decided on its merits. In many countries, for example, smoking is banned in enclosed spaces such as restaurants and cinemas. The usual justification for this is not that it harms the smoker, but that others may suffer ill effects due to inhaling second-hand smoke. More recently, smoking has been banned in public parks, where the risk of inhaling second-hand smoke is negligible; but now the argument is that in parks, children may see people smoking and may try to emulate them, suffering health problems as a result.

There may well be some such risk; but classical liberals question whether risks like this are serious enough to warrant using coercive force to prevent them – or whether they are so infinitesimal that forcible restraint (or fines and other punishments) cannot possibly be justified. For if even infinitesimal risks to others are seen as good reasons for the state to intervene, no human action at all would be protected from the arbitrary intervention of the authorities. There would be no 'private sphere'; and individual freedom and the rule of law would cease to exist.

Toleration has to be conscious. It exists for a reason: namely, that respect for others as moral beings, and respect for their freedoms, is the foundation of peaceful cooperation in a free society. Yet so often our politicians and officials are not conscious of when they are crossing that crucial line. The public also, when problems occur, frequently call for the government to 'do something', even where state intervention would be an unjustifiable assault on individual freedom. And we are also too ready to coerce people 'for their own good' – when in reality we are forcing them only to conform to our own values and prejudices.

'Though we no longer presume to coerce men for their spiritual good', wrote the English philosopher and anthropologist Herbert Spencer (1820–1903), 'we still think ourselves called upon to coerce them for their material good: not seeing that the one is as useless and as unwarrantable as the other'. That is just one reason why classical liberals call for limits on government.

# 6   CLASSICAL LIBERAL POLITICS

## The origin and purpose of government

The early classical liberals believed that government existed solely to protect people's rights, and to expand their opportunity and freedom by minimising coercion and allowing peace to reign. If anyone was to use force, it should be only the government, and it should be used only for these purposes.

Their vision, in other words, was *limited government* – limited in power and scope, and indeed in legitimacy. Regarding power, they were well aware of how official power could jeopardise freedom, and of the need to contain it. On scope, they insisted that legitimate government is not based on conquest and might, but on the agreement of diverse individuals – whose sole purpose for creating it is to promote their rights, freedoms and opportunities. Concerning *legitimacy*, Locke explains that the authority of government comes from the individuals who accept curbs on their behaviour in return for civil rights. Therefore, government authority cannot exceed the authority that those individuals are empowered to give it. For example, it cannot deny our inalienable rights such as life and liberty.

Another good reason to limit government is the frailty of human nature. People in government are merely people; they are probably neither wiser nor less self-interested than anyone else. But they wield enormous coercive power, including powers to fine and imprison us. It would be unwise to let them wield that power as they please; it should be controlled and limited. Classical liberals distrust absolute authority, even if it carries the backing of the vast majority of people.

## Functions of government

But is this too narrow a view of government? Classical liberals are often caricatured as believing in laissez-faire or a tiny, vestigial *night-watchman state*. And critics say that if everyone had to agree what governments existed for, they would not agree on very much, and would remain stuck in anarchy.

Modern governments go well beyond the scope and power that the early classical liberals were willing to grant them. Even classical liberals today often accept that they might have useful functions beyond upholding Mill's no-harm rule and promoting citizens' freedom. Milton Friedman famously advocated a *negative income tax* to redistribute income from rich to poor, and state-funded *education vouchers*, designed to give poor families access to education.

Adam Smith himself thought that, in addition to protecting the public through defence and the justice system, government should provide public works such as bridges and harbours, and contribute to public education.

But while there may be some useful things that are best done collectively, the question is where to draw the line. That is not helped by the fact that it is often hard to decide exactly when real harm is being done or threatened, or what the exact benefits of an intervention might be.

Mill, for example, though a defender of free speech, thought that his no-harm principle might well justify censorship. He also advocated various duties on individuals in order to help others – such as testifying in court, and ensuring that your children are properly schooled. He saw a role for government in the regulation of trade, working hours, wages and workplace benefits. He advocated social welfare laws to provide work for able-bodied people and provide minimum living standards for others. He thought governments should create infrastructure such as roads and sanitation. And he called for public subsidy of scientific research and the arts. Even small public benefits, he thought, would justify such interventions. Many classical liberals would disagree with all of this.

More recently, and even in a book about excessive state power (*The Road to Serfdom*), F. A. Hayek also listed some of the functions he thought governments might legitimately take on. They included providing people with a minimum of food, shelter and clothing, sufficient to preserve their health and capacity to work; a comprehensive system of social insurance for misfortunes that are difficult to insure against; assisting after natural disasters, for which again individuals cannot prepare; and economic policy to combat business cycles and the unemployment they create.

Many classical liberals worry that concessions like these are the thin end of a very large wedge. As Hayek himself complained, 'emergencies have always been the pretext on which the safeguards of individual liberty have been eroded' – and when we let the state provide emergency relief, food, shelter, clothing, education and healthcare, it is not easy to hold the line between what counts as necessities for the few and conveniences for the many. There is, in other words, no obvious *limit* to such government intervention.

Adam Smith squares the circle by saying that his interventions – bridges, harbours and support for education – are merely the infrastructure that allows human beings to cooperate with each other socially and economically. They therefore *promote* freedom rather than threaten it. Hayek too, sees his interventions as trying to keep people able to fend for themselves; so again, his idea is to provide only what it takes to enable free individuals to live, work and cooperate together.

Nevertheless, *any* government activity, however worthy, requires some assault on people's rights and freedoms – specifically, taking their property, in the form of taxes, to pay for state activities. Some classical liberals, arguing that property is one of the things that government exists to *protect*, find this hard to justify. Others simply want assurance that the public benefit – however it is defined – is large enough to justify the intrusion on individuals' rights and freedoms.

The real-world danger is 'mission creep' – governments starting with a few things that are clearly collective responsibilities, and then expanding their powers and functions, with no obvious end point. Classical liberals are perhaps better qualified to draw the boundary than most, since they understand the need for *limited* government and the dangers of burgeoning government power. And they see why, though government might have a role in making sure that some things such as emergency relief *are provided*, it should not itself *provide* them. They also understand why, though government might *regulate* a market, it should remain an *umpire* and not become a market *player*; and why government-led assistance to particular people and groups in distress should *not* expand into long-term and large-scale income redistribution.

## The myth of social justice

The 'new liberals', by contrast, think that income redistribution is exactly what governments *should* do. They see inequality and poverty as the result of unequal power and unjust property laws that benefit employers and the rich but harm employees and the poor. To promote 'social justice', therefore, government must correct the power imbalance and redirect wealth and income from better off to worse off people.

Classical liberals think this a gross misuse of the word 'justice'. To them, justice is *commutative justice*, the resolution of conflicts between individuals and upholding the rights and freedoms of individuals by punishing those who intrude on them. It is about restraining threats and violence, and granting restitution to people who are made worse off by coercion. It is about the conduct we expect, and have a right to expect, from each other.

Real justice, therefore, focuses solely on how people behave towards each other. Being robbed is unjust; catching flu is a *misfortune* but it is not *unjust*, because nobody has acted unjustly. Social or *distributive justice*, on the other hand, is quite different. It is about the distribution of things between different members of a group. It seeks to alter that distribution – generally towards greater equality – even if the existing distribution is simply the outcome of events, and nobody has behaved badly or acted unjustly.

If, for example, 100,000 people each pay to watch a popular singer at a stadium, they end the evening slightly poorer and the singer ends it significantly richer. But nobody has done anything wrong, and nobody has been coerced. Classical liberals would therefore ask: how can the resulting distribution of wealth possibly be *unjust*? And they point out that to return things to equality would *require coercion* – taking the singer's new wealth by force in order to return it to the audience. Indeed, as Nozick says, it would require *constant and repeated coercion* to maintain that equality over the future.

There are practical problems too. Complete equality of income is impossible: why should people bother to work hard, or work at all, if they get paid the same as those who do not? So 'social justice' focuses more on redistribution according to *need*, or in proportion to the *value* that people deliver to society. But who is to decide who is in need, and whose value is greatest? Is someone who becomes poor out of sheer laziness less 'needy' than someone whose home and business is destroyed in a typhoon? Does a nurse contribute more to society than a violinist? There is no objective way to judge: the decision is entirely subjective. Yet, on the back of such arbitrary judgements, the advocates of 'social justice' take people's property and freedom.

Not only that, but 'social justice' treats people differently: people pay different amounts of tax, or receive different amounts of state support, depending on how rich or poor they are. This offends against the rule of law – the principle that the law should treat people equally and that nobody should be helped or harmed by arbitrary rulings by the authorities.

Classical liberals, therefore, reject any comprehensive redistribution of wealth or income. They may advocate some temporary state-organised emergency relief; but they deny that anyone has a *right* to long-term welfare support – because that implies that others have an *obligation* to support them, under compulsion if necessary, even though they share no blame for the unfortunate circumstances of their fellow citizens.

This does not mean that poorer people fare badly in a classical liberal society. Free societies tend to be richer societies, and it is better to be poor in a rich country than in a destitute one. People in rich countries also tend to contribute more through charitable giving and philanthropic works; though they have no legal obligation to help others in need, they have the resources to back up the moral obligation they feel towards them.

## Public choice and private interests

Classical liberals are in any case highly suspicious of how the political decisions on matters such as redistribution are made. Their doubts have been underpinned by the work of the Public Choice School, which applied economic concepts to the political decision-making process, and found it seriously wanting.

Mainstream 'welfare economists' long talked about *market failure* and the need for government action to correct it. What they forgot is that there is *government failure* too. Politicians and officials are not angels: there is as much self-interest in the democratic system as there is in the private marketplace.

Elections, for example, are battles of competing interests, in which the majority decide what should be done. That is a big threat to the minority – like the old joke about democracy being two wolves and a sheep deciding what to have for dinner. It is made worse by the fact that elections are dominated by lobby groups, who campaign vigorously to win electoral benefits for their highly concentrated interests. Often, interest groups will create mutually supporting coalitions to make their electoral leverage even greater. Politicians, meanwhile, have to appease these coalitions of vested interests in order to win their votes – after all, even the most public-spirited politician has to get elected in order to do anything. The people who lose out, of course, are the 'silent majority' – the general public, whose interests are much more diffuse.

Nor are decisions in the legislature any prettier. In order to get their own measures through, legislators engage their colleagues in rounds of 'you vote for my measure, and I will vote for yours'. So more laws are passed than anyone really wants, and the unrepresented general public are exploited even more. And when these laws are implemented, the bureaucracy again has its own interests – perhaps adding to the size and complexity of programmes in order to expand their own empires.

## Classical liberalism and democracy

Classical liberals are democrats, but *sceptical democrats*. They accept that there are some minimal functions that require collective action. They believe that the general public, not some powerful elite, should make the broad decisions on what those functions are and how to achieve them. And they suggest that representative government is probably the best way to make and implement those decisions.

But they know that the democratic process is far from perfect. It is not a process that *reconciles different interests* (as markets do), but one in which we *choose between conflicting interests* – a choice in which only one side can win. It is scarred by the self-interest of electors, of representatives and of officials; it can produce deeply irrational results; and all too often it leads to minority groups being exploited, and their liberties curbed, all in the name of 'democracy'.

For these reasons, classical liberals maintain that democratic decision-making should be bound by certain rules, and should focus, with precision, on those issues that cannot be decided in any other way. Representative democracy is certainly the best form of government yet devised, which makes many people (and almost all of those who happen to be in power) argue that more and more things should be decided through the democratic process. But that means deciding them through the *political* process; and politics is not always a benign force. The more things that are decided politically, the easier it becomes for the rights and liberties of individuals to be eroded, and for minority groups to be exploited or suppressed by those who are wield the coercive power of the state.

To a classical liberal, by contrast, rights and freedoms are for everyone: they are not a matter of numbers and majorities. Genuine representative democracy is not the same as elected dictatorship, and should not be allowed to mutate into it. Election success does not license the winning majority to treat other people exactly as it chooses.

As well as limiting the democratic – political – process to deciding issues that have to be decided and can only be decided collectively, classical liberals would also endeavour to protect the rights and freedoms of all individuals by imposing restraints on how the process is conducted and how such decisions are made.

## Constitutions and freedom

A constitution is one way of setting out those restraints, and giving them force that cannot be easily overridden by those who happen to be in the majority and in power at the time. This does not always succeed: even countries with seemingly strong liberal constitutions are not immune from rapid increases in the size of government and from the erosion of individual rights and liberties by majorities. Constitutional freedoms are hard to protect if the general public loses its understanding of their importance and its will to protect them.

But classical liberals generally believe that setting up constitutional restraints gives us the best chance of protecting individual rights and freedoms.

Through rules such as the *separation of powers* and *checks and balances* – for example, multi-cameral government, a federal system and judicial review – we can try to prevent vested interest groups capturing the entire decision-making process.

And a classical liberal constitution would not only ensure that government power was limited and divided. It would ensure that laws applied equally to everyone, so that no particular interest groups – including politicians and government officials themselves – could be given special treatment.

Such a constitution might also delineate the boundaries of state power by setting out the basic rights of individuals, over which the state has no authority (because its founding citizens cannot transfer to the state an authority to injure the rights of others that they themselves do not have). But while such a *Bill of Rights* might helpfully remind everyone of basic rights such as life, liberty, property and freedom of contract, thought and speech, it cannot possibly enumerate *every* right and freedom. As Hobbes put it, we should be free to do anything within the 'silence of the law' – but a legal system that tried to list everything we *could* do, rather than the few things we *could not*, would be long, complex, flawed and painfully restrictive.

Rather, there should be a general presumption that people are free to pursue their own ends by any peaceful means, subject only to a few exceptions set out in the law. There is no need to spell out our numerous freedoms, most of which are implicit in the general presumption of freedom.

## The legitimacy of government

As the Swiss–French writer and politician Benjamin Constant (1767–1830) noted, constitutions do not exist to empower our leaders, but to restrain them. None of us has any entitlement to rule over any other; it must be a matter of consent. And if government loses the consent of the public, it loses its entire authority, and its coercive power becomes illegitimate.

That should itself keep government limited, as Frank Knight reminded us: we would never be able to agree on any extensive collection of powers. But governments are also restrained by the threat of rebellion – and quite rightly too, according to Locke and Paine.

Nevertheless, given the coercive force at their disposal, even the most unjust governments can still survive a very long time. Elections, for all their faults, are a more peaceful way of removing governments. Like constitutions, they exist not for choosing our leaders, but for restraining them. That safety valve is critically important: for as classical liberals insist, individuals should not be subject to the arbitrary decisions of others, even of a hugely popular government.

# 7 CLASSICAL LIBERAL SOCIETY

Since classical liberals are suspicious of government power, it is fair to ask them how society should then be organised. In fact, they have a coherent explanation of how society organises itself, without needing central authority – the idea of *spontaneous order.*

## Spontaneous orders

*Spontaneous order* is an old idea. It certainly goes back as far as the French philosopher Montesquieu (1689–1755), who explained how self-interested individuals could unintentionally create a generally beneficial social order; the Scottish Enlightenment scholar Adam Ferguson (1723–1816) talked of social institutions as 'the result of human action, but not of human design' – an idea that Adam Smith described as the 'invisible hand'.

More recently, Hayek updated the idea. He noted that we tend to divide the world into *natural* and *artificial* – imagining *natural* things as wild, irrational, unstructured and disorderly, and *artificial* things as planned, rational, structured and methodical – and simply presume that the latter is preferable.

But, says Hayek, there is another category of things that are orderly, but are not planned or deliberate. Examples are the V-formation of migrating geese, or the complex societies of bees or termites. These social structures are not consciously designed by the creatures involved, but are the orderly consequence of their individual behaviour.

Such spontaneous orders are found in human society too. We have *language*, for example: our complex language and grammar was never deliberately designed by anyone, it simply grew because it was useful. (It is interesting that Esperanto, deliberately designed to be a pan-European language, never caught on, while the other, spontaneous languages of Europe still flourish.)

The *common law*, similarly, was never intentionally created, as the legal code of Napoleon was; it simply emerged from thousands of rulings in individual cases. *Markets, prices* and *money* also developed because they are useful, not because anyone consciously invented them.

The conclusion is that social orders do not need government, or planning, to be functional, efficient or even rational. They emerge through the free interaction of individuals, each pursuing their own private aims but respecting the rights and freedoms of others. Indeed, government intervention is more likely to turn that order into chaos.

## The evolution of spontaneous orders

Spontaneous orders *evolve*. Language, common law, morals, customs and markets all change and adapt to the needs of the time. Such orders are self-organising and generally self-regulating – requiring a few broad rules to keep them working well, but not needing anyone to design and plan them.

They may not adapt perfectly all the time, but the ones that adapt well will survive and prosper better than others. And that trial-and-error evolutionary progress will be much faster when individuals are free to produce their own ideas in abundance than when only the authorities' ideas prevail.

Consider, for example, the throng in a busy railway station, all rushing between their different trains and the different exits and entrances. Somehow, everyone gets to their destination without bumping into each other. That is because they each adjust their direction to take account of others getting in their way. Their eventual route between train and doorway may be very far from a straight line, but generally they get there quickly and without incident. The alternative – to direct those thousands by asking their destination and then plotting their most efficient routes through the station – would be a management nightmare. But luckily the problem solves itself, quite spontaneously.

## Rules and order

The problems described above solve themselves because we adapt to others in predictable ways – in the station case, trying to avoid collisions by subtly indicating where we are heading and adjusting to others' indications too. Such behavioural regularities, or 'rules of conduct', produce a spontaneous, beneficial result. If, by contrast, we all behaved unpredictably, it would create only confusion and conflict.

In real-world spontaneous orders, these 'rules' may not be written down and may well be very complex. Bees, for example, have no writing or command structure, yet they sustain thriving colonies of 50,000 or more simply through the structured labours of each individual.

Regarding human orders, schoolchildren will attest that the rules of grammar, on which our language is built, are very hard to describe, even though we use them unthinkingly every day. The same is true of the rules of justice, or fair play, or morality; we can sense when the rules have been breached, even though we cannot always explain what they are.

But then these order-promoting rules have evolved because they are useful and adaptive, not because we have consciously designed them. They put voluntary limits on our actions, making them more predictable, so easing social life. Rules such as property rights, traditions, customs, morals, honesty, respect and habit are the fire basket that contains the fire of individual freedom. Nobody *invented* them, yet they contain an unconscious 'wisdom' about how to behave in order to promote smooth social interaction.

## Justice and the rule of law

Spontaneous order, then, rests on predictable individual behaviour and would be impossible without it. And the basis of our social or political order, say classical liberals, is the *rules of justice*.

Like grammar, the rules of justice are not consciously designed, but evolve because they are useful; and broadly we follow them, even though we cannot always explain precisely what they are. We do, of course, *try* to write them down and codify them in law books. But that is not us *creating* the rules of justice; it is us trying to *discover* what they are.

Legislators can pass 'laws', but they may not be just laws. For example, they may be *retrospective* (punishing people for actions that were not criminal at the time), or *infeasible* (impossible to comply with), or *incomprehensible* (contradictory or too complicated to understand), or *unfairly enforced* – all of which offend the idea of justice that has grown up with us, or as some classical liberals would say, offend the *natural law*. Such pieces of legislation are therefore unworthy of the name 'law'.

## The rule of law

Classical liberals believe that a spontaneous, cooperative, predictable, non-violent, stable and fair social order arises only by following rules that are *general* (without a bewildering mass of exceptions), *universal* (applying to everyone) and *stable* (not changing so often that people get confused about what they are).

Since most of us could not explain the rules of grammar, never mind the rules of social life, it makes sense to keep things simple. Having rules that are *general* and *stable* means that everyone knows what is expected of them, making our actions more predictable, and allowing us to make plans with greater confidence. So do rules that are *universal* – with the further, crucial advantage that they make it impossible for particular people or groups to be favoured or exploited.

This is the *rule of law*, in contrast to the arbitrary rule of those in authority. Classical liberals stress that it prevents politicians, police, courts and other officials abusing their coercive power. It spares us from many common evils: arbitrary arrest, imprisonment without trial, double jeopardy (being tried multiple times for the same offence), unfair trials, biased judges, rigged elections and unjust legislation.

## Protecting the rule of law

Though classical liberals believe in *limited* government, they see maintaining the rule of law as no *small* task. It requires mechanisms to ensure that elections and appointments are open and fair, that judges remain independent, and that the generality and universality of laws are scrutinised. That requires committing resources to the justice system: justice is not served, for example, if it takes years for cases to get to trial because the court bureaucracy is overwhelmed, or if police and judges are so badly paid that they rely on taking bribes instead.

*Constitutions* can help protect this natural justice: they can enshrine the *due process* of the legal system, to ensure equal treatment; and they can define a *personal sphere* into which legislation and officialdom can never intrude. The *common law* tradition is another bastion of freedom:

individual cases are aired and considered in court, and from that we grow our understanding of what the rules of justice actually are. A third protection is *free speech*: if people can openly criticise legislation and the administration of justice, more thought will go into legislating, and people can actively object to unjust legislation and unjust legal processes.

## Threats to the rule of law

This is all very far from the view of many legislators today. They want the courts to defer to the elected majority, who, they say, are more in touch with public concerns than are judges. They ignore constitutional limits, arguing that they understand present circumstances better than the constitution-writers of decades or centuries ago. They see rights not as natural and inviolable, but as privileges granted to us by the legislature. And they believe that legislation should promote the 'public good' even at the cost of individual liberty.

But almost any legislation, however unjust and coercive, can be excused on the grounds of 'public good' – which, inevitably, is defined by the legislators themselves. And, far from being out of touch, classical liberals see the courts as crucial guardians of individual rights and freedoms, checking the short-termism and vested interests of the legislators, striking down unjust legislation and ensuring that just laws are obeyed, even by those in power.

It is for this reason that Hayek argued strongly that the common law, which grew up through disputes being argued in the courts, was a better guarantee of justice than laws passed by politicians – and most classical liberals would agree. To them, the rule of law demands that legal rules should apply justly and uniformly to everyone. While the common law generally fits this description, too often the laws made by politicians are designed to favour (or disfavour) particular groups – one of the reasons why classical liberals are so sceptical of such legislation.

## The rationality of natural orders

Though many people imagine that a society without central direction must be wild and irrational, classical liberals believe that spontaneous orders are actually *more* rational. They are able to process and use far more information than centralised societies, leading to better decision making, quicker adjustment to changing circumstances, and more rapid progress. (For illustration, recall the economic backwardness of the old, centrally directed Soviet bloc, compared with its less centralised Western neighbours.)

The reason, according to F. A. Hayek, who worked out the details of this line of thought, is that most of the knowledge on which social progress depends is *dispersed knowledge*. It is local, personal, fragmented and partial, and cannot be centralised.

Ordinary people have a better grasp of their own circumstances than central authorities could ever do. They also have specialist skills, and more personal understanding of their particular market and of their customers' needs and values. And much of the changing market information they process would be out of date even before it could be transmitted to some central planning agency.

Some might argue that apps such as Über, and modern supercomputers, do make it possible to collect and process rapidly changing market data such as the fluctuating demand for and the availability of taxis at any particular time and place. It is true that the scale upon which information can be efficiently collected and used will change over time and between uses. But, a process of competition is needed to discover the best way of collecting, interpreting and using information given the available technology. And this information is processed and used in different ways by different people in the process chain – Über or the taxi company, drivers and customers. Central planning simply could not replicate this.

In any event, the problem is not one of *computing* but of *understanding*. The data would certainly not be processed any *better* by a government central authority. No government authority could forecast taxi customers' demand (which changes constantly due to things like family emergencies, the weather or public transport delays). Nor could we expect central planners to have the same in-depth knowledge that taxi drivers have of things like the local weather, temporary road closures and ways round them, local events that attract large crowds, and countless other factors that affect the market.

Also, local suppliers have a much more urgent interest in adapting rapidly to local demand than do central planners. Their motivation drives progress: with thousands of suppliers all vying for business, innovation will be more rapid than it would be if left to a single central agency. And it is better that innovation should be done by individuals: if their innovations do not work, they can be abandoned with only modest, local losses; whereas a nationwide innovation by a central planning agency risks disaster for the whole economy.

It is not that the spontaneous society is unplanned: on the contrary, it relies on the plans of millions of individuals, each with their own specialist knowledge, rather than on some single planning body. Such a society, based on a vast amount of dispersed individual knowledge, is so complex that no central mind could ever comprehend it. This explains, in part, classical liberals' suspicion of government power, particularly of attempts to redesign society wholesale. If we cannot fully understand our social institutions, we are unlikely to be able to redesign them with any success.

## Civil society

Classical liberals do not imagine that the people who comprise the spontaneous society are isolated, *atomistic* individuals (though there were hints of this among the early social contract theorists, and more recently in the economists' notions of *rational expectations* and of the rational, self-interested *homo economicus*). They know that people in the real world are not detached and mechanical.

Rather, by choice or birth, individuals are members of different, overlapping groups, with different family, moral, religious, cultural and other allegiances. Their values are influenced by these allegiances, and they rely on the mutual loyalty of their fellow members. They pursue their ambitions less through the political process than through these institutions of *civil society* – charities, unions, self-help groups, campaigns, religions and many other groupings.

Communists and fascists are highly critical of civil society because they see it as diverting people's allegiances away from the state. Classical liberals cherish the idea of civil society for precisely the same reason. To them, civil society enables individuals to pursue their own goals without being subservient to a powerful, centralised political authority. Indeed, different people can pursue mutually contradictory purposes, without having to sacrifice their ambitions to some majority view. Furthermore, there is less excuse for governments to take on additional powers if civil society is strong. A lively charitable sector, for example, means there is less need to create a state welfare system – a relief to classical liberals, because they fear the growth and potential abuse of centralised power. And it is more rational for tasks to be undertaken locally and in a variety of different ways, than to be attempted by distant, centralised authority.

Some classical liberals welcome civil society as sparing us, not just from the dangers of excessive centralisation, but from the dangers of excessive individualism too. For example, the French political thinker and historian Alexis de Tocqueville (1805–59) criticised the individualism of America for smothering civic virtue and restraint, creating the possibility of tyranny by the masses, backed up by the power of the state.

## Spontaneous order and natural rights

It may be worth noting the conflict between the ideas of spontaneous order and natural rights. If society develops spontaneously, no social contract between isolated, free individuals is needed to explain it. It is not the product of rational negotiation, but the entirely unintended, evolutionary consequence of individuals adapting to each other's actions.

To many classical liberals, this suggests a less radical, more conservative approach to social issues than does the natural rights approach. One of the criticisms of the natural rights view is that it might produce something near anarchy, since there is probably very little that discrete individuals, jealously guarding their natural rights, would actually agree on, leaving almost no role for government at all. The spontaneous order approach, by contrast, suggests that we can and do agree on a great deal – even if our agreement is unconscious and scarcely understood.

## 8 CLASSICAL LIBERAL ECONOMICS

## The spontaneous order of the market

Alongside social and political freedom, classical liberals also advocate *economic* freedom. They believe people should be free to invent, create, save, accumulate property and exchange things voluntarily with others.

But they also believe that economic freedom is the best way to create general prosperity. That is because economic freedom allows people to adjust spontaneously to each other's needs and cooperate for their mutual benefit – creating and spreading value in the process.

The rules that create this particular spontaneous order are those of property, contract, honesty and justice. Between them, they create an economic order of incomprehensible scale and complexity – far larger and more complex than any conscious agency could grasp, embracing the whole world.

## The spontaneous 'miracle' of prices

What keeps the economic activities of so many millions of people in such remarkably smooth adjustment is what Hayek called the 'miracle' of the price system. We did not invent this – it emerged spontaneously, yet it drives the creation of value and spreads prosperity throughout the human community.

Prices are simply the *rates* at which people are willing to exchange some things for others. Usually they are expressed in money – but that is only because money has emerged as a useful good that can be exchanged for other things. In Milton Friedman's words, it saves hungry barbers having to seek out bakers who need a haircut – making exchange much easier and smoother.

Note that prices do not measure *value*. Value, like beauty, exists in the mind of the beholder, and people value the same things differently. That is why they trade. While hungry barbers value bread more than the amount of money the baker demands for it, the baker values the cash more than the bread. A single *price* is exchanged, but they each *value* things differently, and each consider themselves better off by the trade.

## Prices as telecommunication

But prices do reveal *scarcity*. Higher prices can show where the demand for things is outstripping their supply, such that consumers are prepared to pay more. And they induce suppliers to satisfy that demand by stepping up their production in order to capture the higher rewards on offer. Falling prices, similarly, can indicate that demand is weak and suppliers should cut back production. In this way, prices indicate where resources can create most value, and draw them towards those applications and away from wasteful, less valued uses.

These beneficial adjustments spread out from market to market. Suppose, to take Hayek's example, that manufacturers find some new use for tin. They will then demand more tin, and will be prepared to pay higher prices to obtain it. Those higher prices will induce mining firms to produce more tin, and wholesalers to supply it. But equally, existing users of tin will now start looking for less expensive substitutes. That will bid up the price of those substitutes – which will prompt users of those substitutes to look for other substitutes. A whole series of adjustments spread out, like ripples in a pond – all thanks to what Hayek called the 'vast telecommunications system' of prices, constantly showing people where their effort and resources will generate most value.

## Markets without commands

Unlike the textbook 'equilibrium' diagrams, which suggest that markets stay in constant balance, classical liberals see markets as a dynamic *process*, like a mountain stream, never settling in one place. Instead of imagining 'the economy' as an abstract, mechanical *system*, classical liberals see market phenomena as the unplanned, unpredictable *result* of the constant, mutual adjustment of millions of individual human beings, each with their *own* purposes and values.

This spontaneous economic order is, like others, the result of predictable rules of behaviour among the individuals who comprise it. It is motivated by self-interest and profit, but regulated by factors such as competition, contract, property rights and justice – principles that classical liberals believe the state must uphold in order to keep the market order functioning beneficially.

## Rules and property

Property rights are fundamental to the operation of this beneficial order. People with secure ownership can exchange items of their property with others who value them more – benefiting both sides. Even more profoundly, secure ownership means that people can produce what they are good at producing and exchange it with others for what *they* are good at producing. This specialisation, or *division of labour*, makes us all much more productive than if we tried to do everything, amateurishly, for ourselves.

Secure ownership rights also allow people to *build capital*, investing in tools and equipment that enable them to produce more, faster and better. And they enable people to resist exploitation by political majorities; indeed, they give people the resource to stand up to overweening governments.

### *Property rules*

Property rights enable people to hold and use property, to exclude others from using it, to earn income from it (say, by renting it out) and to transfer it to others by sale or gift. These rights are enforced by the justice system.

But for someone's ownership to be legitimate, property must be acquired without coercion. It might be acquired through trade or gift. Or perhaps by taking something that nobody else owns or wants, such as a piece of wasteland – a process that *injures* nobody, even if the new owner finds profitable use for it.

Property is not just land, buildings and moveable property. It can include complex intangibles, such as shares and bonds, or intellectual property such as patented designs and copyrighted music – and indeed, the property we all have in our own lives and freedoms. It can be held by individuals, organisations, governments, or by no one (sea fisheries, for example) – though classical liberals believe that private owners generally manage property better than government owners, and that ownership by no one risks the 'tragedy of the commons' in which resources are over-exploited because nobody has an owner's interest in conserving them.

The rules of property may be complex, but they enable countless people to cooperate peacefully through specialisation and voluntary exchange. They have evolved precisely because they make that beneficial cooperation possible.

When people have clear and enforceable ownership rights, they are more likely to conserve and invest in a property resource, and maintain it in productive use. That plainly benefits the owner; but it benefits everyone else too. It means the fruits of that investment are available to be traded. That trade, in turn, promotes specialisation, productivity and the spread of value. Contrast that with war-torn or lawless countries in which farmers see no point in planting and tending crops that will be stolen or destroyed by marauding thieves or armies.

## The arguments for economic freedom

Unlike traditional economic approaches, classical liberals do not construct any all-embracing *model* to explain economic phenomena. To them, economic phenomena like prices are the unpredictable *result* of the complex mutual adjustment of millions of individuals. But that does not mean it is random and irrational. On the contrary, market processes contain a great deal of 'wisdom' that has accumulated over long periods of trial and error.

### Personal and dispersed information

In fact, there is *more* wisdom and planning in this arrangement than in any deliberately designed and planned economy, because the free economic order has much more – and more *relevant* – information to work on.

All those millions of individuals have much better knowledge of their own local circumstances, of their own values, and of the priorities of their customers and suppliers, than any distant economic planning agency ever could.

Nor could planners even collect this information. Not only is it vast in scale, dispersed and partial, but it is also *personal*. Skills, experience, a market understanding, a feel for customers' wants – these are the essential knowledge that drives economic life, but which cannot be transmitted to central planners. Should we produce oil or wine? It is not a matter of arithmetical calculation. The only reason we go to the effort of producing things is to consume them, and what people want to consume depends on their needs and values – feelings that cannot be summed or subtracted, that are deeply subjective, and which change from moment to moment depending on countless unpredictable factors.

But the spontaneous economic order is *not* unplanned. On the contrary, it is the result of *continuous planning* by millions of individuals, each using their dispersed, partial and personal knowledge in order to anticipate the wants and needs of others and to plan how to direct resources into satisfying those wants.

## Competition

Economic freedom works because, in the absence of coercion, the only way to promote our own self-interest is to meet the needs and interests of others. Classical liberals see open competition as the key driver of this, because when consumers have a choice of suppliers and products to choose from, producers are spurred to serve their needs as cost-effectively as they can. Real competition is not the bloodless textbook model of 'perfectly' identical suppliers, products and consumers. It is a dynamic and human *process* in which diverse producers strive to differentiate their offerings so as to appeal to diverse customers with many different preferences.

These 'imperfections' are what give markets their dynamism and drive innovation, efficiency and improvement. It is *shortages* and unfulfilled wants – revealed by rising prices – that prompt producers to step in and fill them. It is *surpluses* that tell producers that productive resources are being wasted. It is the variety and diversity of goods on offer that enable the different – and even contradictory – tastes of consumers to be satisfied.

## Public utility

The free economy reconciles people with different values. Buyers and sellers can freely cooperate with each other precisely because they differ in how they value a particular good or service. Through the medium of money, we can even trade with people on the other side of the world, whose values, religion, morality and world-view may be completely different from ours. And arguably, the global economic interdependence of peoples with such diverse views is the most powerful force for peace in human history.

It may be self-interest that motivates individuals, but through property, specialisation, markets and exchange, that self-interest is harnessed for the general benefit. Things are produced more cost-effectively; consumers are served well by the upward pressure on quality and downward pressure on price; new property is created and value is increased; wants are filled; choice is expanded; human diversity and individuality are celebrated.

And even if individuals are motivated by philanthropy, they have the same interest in preserving that same system, which allows them to maximise the value of what they can create and disperse to others.

## The destabilising effects of government

Economic freedom is important to us, and not just because economic activity occupies so much of our waking hours. It is also fundamental to our social and political freedoms. For example, freedom of speech is compromised if those in power control the newspapers, TV, radio and online media. Free association would be threatened if the political authorities owned all the meeting halls. We could not enjoy the fruits of our own labour if the state managed our offices and factories. Classical liberals therefore see economic freedom and private ownership as an essential bulwark against excessive state power.

When countries such as the UK and the US became rich, their governments were much smaller than they are today. Now, nearly all countries have large government establishments that require high taxes to sustain them. Classical liberals see that as an attack on property rights. Modest taxes may be inescapable in order to provide for essential government functions such as defence and justice. But high taxes discourage work and saving, dampen the creative dynamism of markets, and divert resources from highly valued uses to those chosen by (often unrepresentative) political authorities.

Regulation, too, may be needed in order to keep markets free – upholding open competition and countering exploitation, for example. But again, by restraining commercial agreements, regulation can diminish the value that is created out of voluntary exchange. And in any case, many regulations are created to serve political and vested interests, not the general public.

Classical liberals conclude that government intervention in economic life is usually catastrophic. Since taxation is unpopular, governments borrow – taking money from the next generation, without their consent. They let the value of their currency erode, so they can repay their debt in devalued money; but that *inflation* destabilises the price system, drowning the signal of changing relative prices among the noise of generally rising prices, making it harder for people to see where their effort and resources would be most valuably applied. And governments are frequently tempted to manipulate money and interest rates in the hope of stimulating economic booms – a defiance of market realities that invariably ends in busts, unemployment and recession. Classical liberals would much prefer to prohibit these damaging interventions.

## Health, education and welfare without the state

Classical liberals are also sceptical about government involvement in services such as health, education and welfare – which consume most of the government budget in developed countries.

Welfare, for example, aims to eliminate poverty, but arguably does the opposite, adversely tilting the balance between (subsidised) unemployment and (taxed) employment. Most of the leading classical liberal thinkers argue for at least some minimum welfare provision by the state, but they believe that such support is best provided through market mechanisms. For example, they would prefer that people insured themselves against unemployment, sickness and disability, with charities – re-energised by the retreat of the state – helping in hardship cases, or with the state paying the premiums of those who could not afford the cover. This, they say, would be much less wasteful. And it would create more positive incentives, and fewer perverse incentives, than today's state benefit systems, which often promote dependency (both among beneficiaries and among the state bureaucrats who administer the systems).

Healthcare, too, is often government provided or highly regulated, leaving people with no choice of insurer or provider. Since competition works well in other markets, classical liberals ask why it should not work in hospitals too, keeping costs down and quality high – from which the poor, who presently find healthcare unaffordable or inaccessible, would benefit most. And genuinely competitive insurance would make people aware of the potential cost of unhealthy lifestyles, without any need for state hectoring.

Education is often another state monopoly, crowding out alternative providers – and indeed alternative ideas, which can only be harmful in a supposedly free society. So classical liberals argue for competition in schooling, which again would help the poor, trapped in 'sink' schools, the most. Some classical liberals, such as Mill, believe that basic education should still be compulsory, though others insist that there is no need, since schooling is one of parents' highest priorities for their children; and that charities again would solve cases of hardship.

## Trade and protectionism

Classical liberals maintain that international trade should be just as free as domestic commerce. That allows countries to specialise in what they do well; and it allows consumers to enjoy goods from all over the world. Historically, countries that have been open to trade, such as Hong Kong, have grown most quickly; and the recent opening up of trade with countries such as China and India has taken billions of people out of abject poverty.

International trade, classical liberals argue, spreads international cooperation, tolerance and ideas. Yet, motivated by politics, far too many nations try to protect their own producers with import quotas and tariffs. This prevents potential importers benefitting from the fruits of their own labour, and means less choice for consumers, less specialisation, less efficient use of resources, and a loss of value. It also leads to tit-for-tat retaliation, trade wars and international tension. But this occurs only because governments encroach too readily on free economic activity.

# 9 CLASSICAL LIBERALISM TODAY

## Eclipse and revival
### The decline of classical liberalism

Classical liberalism flourished in the seventeenth and eighteenth centuries; and to it we owe much of the great era of free trade and economic growth of the nineteenth. But by the late nineteenth century, other ideas were beginning to take hold. Industrialisation, one of the products of economic freedom, brought social problems – family upheavals, a rapid move to the towns, and a greater perception of inequality now that people were living closer together.

By the twentieth century, industrial society became a recruiting ground for socialism, communism and then national socialism, complete with the militarism that goes with centralising ideologies. But rather than rejecting centralism after the inevitable conflicts, the post-war victors concluded that their own centralised command structures could help them 'win the peace' just as it had 'won the war'.

There was also by then a greater confidence in our economic understanding. Economists believed that they had the knowledge, and the tools, to control employment and output, and that central planning would prove effortlessly superior to the supposed 'irrationality' of the market.

## The unravelling consensus

Though it seemed an age at the time, it did not take long for this view to discredit itself. Improved travel and communications showed up the economic, social and political shortcomings of the communist bloc. West Germany boomed after the 'bonfire of controls' lit by Ludwig Erhard one Sunday morning in 1948 – while East Germany, on the other side of the infamous Berlin Wall, became steadily grimmer. The same happened in the two Koreas once the peninsula was split into free and communist segments. A more educated and enlightened world population came to see militarism not as its protection but as a threat to its growing economic interdependence.

Post-war economic policy was creaking too. The expansionist policies of British economist John Maynard Keynes (1883–1946), designed for a time of depression, turned the peace dividend into a burgeoning expansion of government and a raging inflation – inexplicably, for Keynesians, accompanied by unemployment and stagnation.

# The rebirth of classical liberalism

For classical liberals, all this was far from inexplicable. As Hayek would explain, it revealed the 'fatal conceit' of imagining that we could manipulate the spontaneous order of social and economic life at our pleasure.

Though consigned to the intellectual wilderness, classical liberals regrouped to take stock and think through their ideas and make them relevant to the modern era. The fightback started in April 1947, when Hayek assembled a small group of European and American classical liberal thinkers in the mountains above Lake Geneva, at the first meeting of what would become the Mont Pelerin Society. Its members would go on to found classical liberal think tanks such as the Institute of Economic Affairs, from which many others would spring.

Several members, including Hayek himself, would win Nobel prizes for their contribution to the classical liberal economic revival: laureates George Stigler (1911–91), Milton Friedman (1912–2006) and Gary Becker (1930–2014), for example, would become leading lights of the Chicago School of Economics, with its emphasis on sound money, limited government and market freedom; while their fellow laureate James M. Buchanan (1919–2013) would lead the Public Choice School attack on the supposed rationality of government decision making. By the end of the twentieth century, their ideas were motivating the leading governments of the world.

## The meaning of classical liberalism

One thing that contemporary classical liberals have failed at, however, is finding a good name for themselves. The qualifier 'classical' harks back to the age of Locke and Smith: and while there was much wisdom in their ideas, the world has changed, and contemporary classical liberals have developed their thinking in new ways to deal with current situations and arguments.

Unfortunately for them, though, the plain term 'liberal' has been captured (at least in America, though the confusion spreads out from there) by those who champion civil rights and political freedom, but who are suspicious of economic freedom and private ownership, and believe that the state has a big role to play in righting past wrongs and promoting equality. The terms 'new liberal' and 'modern liberal' have also been annexed.

The word 'neo-liberal' might have served, had it not become a mere term of abuse used by the critics of contemporary classical liberalism. The word originated among the 'Ordo-liberal' promoters of West Germany's post-war 'social market economy'. But more recently is has been used to create a caricature, in which classical liberals are seen as single-minded economic fanatics, with no social conscience or thought for the needy, defending every action of business, and demanding laissez-faire and a night-watchman state – if any. Such a straw man is very easy to attack but, as we have seen, all this is very far from what classical liberals actually believe.

## The classical liberal spectrum

However, classical liberalism is not a set ideology; rather, as we have seen, it is a spectrum of approaches to the questions of social, economic and political freedom. Beyond one end are anarchists (and some libertarians), who see no necessity for state institutions at all. Beyond the other end are conservatives, who believe that the state has a powerful role, not just in defending basic rights, but in preserving certain moral or political values.

Classical liberals put more emphasis on culture, representative government and the rules underpinning the spontaneous economic and social order than do libertarians; yet they are less willing than conservatives to sacrifice freedom to social utility, even though many of them stress social utility as important.

But again, different classical liberals are motivated by different core principles. For some, like Friedman, freedom is important, but the consequences of freedom are what really counts; they favour deregulation, privatisation and lower taxes not just because they enhance freedom, but for the beneficial social outcomes they produce. Others, like Hayek, see free action, restrained by certain moral and legal rules, as an essential underpinning of the spontaneous order. Yet others, like Nozick, insist that human beings all have immutable natural rights that leave hardly any legitimate role for the state, except in rectifying injustice.

But despite their diverse views, classical liberals do agree on basic principles. They believe that the key purpose of the state is to *safeguard our rights* to life, liberty, property and our pursuit of happiness. Since that is such an important function, the state might not turn out so small, but if we are to protect our freedoms against the abuse of state power, it has to be limited in scope. Classical liberals believe *voluntary exchange* is the best way to add and spread value, unleash our creative spirit and celebrate our diversity and self-expression. They have an *antipathy to absolutism* in political, economic or social life, yet maintain that we do need some moral and legal rules to preserve the smooth operation of spontaneous social and economic orders. They believe that individuals should *take responsibility* for their actions: while we are free to help others and often do, nobody has any *right* to demand support from anyone else. But they grant all human individuals *equal moral status*, and *equal treatment under the law*.

## Classical liberal internationalism

Classical liberals are internationalist in their beliefs, regarding the whole of humanity as sharing in basic rights and freedoms. But they nurse no Utopian idea of world government, or even world civil society. Realistically, they accept that citizens are highly attached to their own nation states; and they seek only to educate them and to defuse conflict between those states. That is something that international travel and economic interdependence can help with greatly – spreading ideas, opportunities, choices and freedom at the same time.

Classical liberals believe that the principles of freedom that apply in any nation should be matched internationally, in principles such as freedom of trade, capital and migration across borders, and non-discrimination against foreigners or their goods, services and property. But, as the German Ordo-liberal Wilhelm Röpke (1899–1966) put it, internationalism begins at home. If we maintain just laws, freedoms and the rule of law within our own nation states, there is then at least some possibility that the same principles will inform our international dealings and institutions. Classical liberals have no imperialist ambitions for their ideas: empires are no way to win people's minds, though they often suppress their thoughts. Classical liberals welcome diversity between cultures and countries as they do between communities, families and individuals.

## Dealing with illiberal groups

An interesting problem for classical liberals, however, is how they should deal with groups and nations that are highly *illiberal*. The problem has become more urgent. There have always been religious and political fundamentalists who reject any idea of political, social and economic freedom and who would gladly extinguish our own freedoms if they had the reach to do so. But now, with travel so easy and destructive technologies so obtainable, the potential threat has become more dangerous.

Classical liberals have generally favoured toleration over intervention, which they see as conflicting with people's rights of self-determination. But if other groups or states have set their goal as destroying freedom and toleration itself, the question is how much intolerance classical liberals can tolerate. Mill, writing in the nineteenth century, argued that we had every right to intervene in 'barbarian' states, but not 'civilised' ones, since only 'civilised' states were on a moral par with us; and, in any event, it was unlikely that intervention into the affairs of 'civilised' states would change them. Much more recently, John Rawls used a similar argument, that we could tolerate 'decent' but not 'outlaw' states.

In typical fashion, classical liberals maintain a range of views on such issues, some stressing self-determination, the robustness of free societies against illiberal assaults, and the pointless cost of trying to change people's religious beliefs; others arguing that we should intervene for our own defence. The latter strategy opens up another question, of how to identify when a group or nation is truly illiberal and how much of a threat it is. China, for example, has no political and little social freedom, but a fair measure of economic freedom; while its economic and military power unnerves many. Does that make it a threat to classical liberal nations?

## Illiberalism at home

Similar issues arise over the question of how to deal with illiberal groups at home. Classical liberals worry that intervention (such as banning particular religious or political groups) is at odds with their own core principles, and undermines the autonomy and self-expression of other people. They are mostly disposed to tolerate religious and political groups, though in some cases (the rise of national socialism in Germany, for example) may wish that they had not.

On the other hand, many classical liberals would think it right to intervene to prevent girls being denied an education, for example, or to prevent female genital mutilation and forced marriages. These are seen as breaches of the rights and freedoms enjoyed by all human beings.

Classical liberals have no prescriptive answer to such questions. But in general they take the view that state action should be kept to a minimum. Some take the view that we live in a pluralist age, and are mature enough to tolerate different manners and customs, so intervention is generally not justified unless there is some overwhelming 'public' case for doing so. Others emphasise that persuasion and debate are more effective at changing minds in the long run. A law against female genital mutilation, for example, is probably less effective at ending this practice than women who have undergone it being free to decide not to inflict it on their own children. It is that freedom that the law should be defending.

Once again, what would classical liberals do if illiberal groups found themselves in the ascendant and used their political power to strip away people's rights and freedoms? To some, like Paine, that would be justification enough to rise up and overthrow such a government. But realistically, classical liberals know that things would have to come to a sorry pass before something like that happened.

## The classical liberal vision

Classical liberals have no illusions about the world. Human beings are not perfect; their world cannot be explained by pure principles, nor managed by simple equations. Events are usually the unpredictable result of the actions, but not always the intentions, of human beings who are often less than rational and far from beneficent. Our best policy is to admit all this, and to harness human frailty in ways that promote human benefit, such as free markets.

Classical liberalism is, as we saw at the outset, a humane idea. It accepts people as the diverse human beings they are. It seeks to maximise the space and opportunity they have to pursue their different objectives. And it seeks ways in which the citizens of so diverse a world can cooperate peacefully together.

Classical liberals want a world at peace, with a minimum of coercion (and that itself exercised only by legitimate and representative governments). They want the world to enjoy the prosperity generated by voluntary exchange within a free economic order, and want legal systems that protect the rights of all human beings and enable them to adjust cooperatively to each other's ambitions.

They want limits on power, seeing the might of governments as a cause of international conflict and domestic repression. They demand a rule of law that curbs arbitrary power and makes our rulers subject to the same laws as everyone else. They support the freedom of everyone to think, speak, work and pursue their own aims, provided that they do not harm others in the process, and they stress the importance of an independent justice system to maintain that order. They support people's freedom to pursue their own ends in their own way, even if it is self-destructive, and do not want anyone to have to ask some authority for permission before doing something. And, crucially, they want to designate a personal sphere where the political authorities have no right to interfere with us at all.

Classical liberals are confident about the free economic order. They maintain that its gradual expansion across the world has brought better education, higher life expectancy, greater longevity, freedom from disease and more opportunity, particularly to the poorest. This started to happen long before socialism and interventionism became rife, and it can be seen spreading now to countries in poorer regions that are at last opening up to market ideas and international trade – allowing people everywhere to sell the fruits of their labour to distant markets, boosting the specialisation and efficiency of producers in different countries, creating and spreading value. With the price system prompting people to fill unfilled wants and needs, classical liberals believe there are no logical limits to economic growth and human prosperity. Innovation, improvement and the effort of every person to better their condition will remain as uniform, constant and uninterrupted as legislators and regulators permit.

## A classical liberal world?

Are we already living in such a world? Hardly: in an age of complexity, uncertainty, volatility and diversity, many people still look to governments for protection and economic security. And as governments grow, the public choice problem grows even more. The more resources that are controlled by governments, the more worthwhile it is for interest groups to demand favours, and the more essential it is for politicians to appease them.

Countries may have recognised, at last, the failures of public ownership and privatised their state industries; but outright ownership has been replaced by burgeoning regulation. Politicians may not be patricians any more, but they are no less patronising, passing lifestyle laws supposedly to save us from ourselves.

Classical liberals have still not succeeded in making those in power understand the limits of their legitimate authority; and why would the powerful want to limit themselves anyway? But there is no doubt that support for economic, political and social freedom is spreading throughout the world, thanks in large part to improved travel, education and communications. Classical liberalism may still draw upon the heritage of Locke, but one of its joys is that it does not try to shoehorn humanity into some defunct model; rather, it aims to unleash the infinite optimism and adaptability of the world.

# 10 KEY CLASSICAL LIBERAL THINKERS

## John Locke (1632–1704), English philosopher

Many consider Locke the founding father of classical liberalism. After exile in France because of his hostility to the Stuart monarchy, he wrote his *Two Treatises of Civil Government* (1690), justifying the overthrow of James II, scorning the 'divine right' of kings and asserting that legitimate government is based on a contract with the people, not 'force and violence'. In a state of nature, he speculated, people have every right to preserve their own lives, health and property – which they acquire by 'mixing their labour' with natural resources – against incursion by others. To protect these *natural rights* peacefully, they contract to form governments that they empower to preserve them. Government therefore gets its legitimacy from the consent of the governed; if it fails to protect their rights, they are justified in overthrowing it. These ideas strongly influenced the American and French revolutions, and constitutional thinkers such as Thomas Jefferson (1743–1826).

## Bernard Mandeville (1670–1733), Anglo–Dutch satirist

Mandeville's satirical poem *The Grumbling Hive* (1705), re-published as *The Fable of the Bees* (1714), shocked readers by suggesting that self-interest drove industry, commerce, prosperity and social harmony. In his imaginary hive, the bees are interested only in themselves, but in satisfying their desires, they create employment for others; and when they spend, purely for self-gratification, they unintentionally enrich others and spread wealth through the community. This idea of a spontaneous economic order based on self-interest underpinned the 'invisible hand' model of Adam Smith (1723–90) and was later elaborated by Friedrich Hayek (1899–1992).

## Voltaire [François-Marie Arouet] (1694–1778), French writer

Exiled from France by aristocratic laws, Voltaire went to England and was attracted by its civil liberties, its constitutional government, and its classical liberal thinking. He decided to dedicate his life to the promotion of basic freedoms, tolerance, free speech and free trade. His *Philosophical Letters on the English* (1734) criticised the illiberalism of France; he urged the overthrow of aristocratic powers and criticised the intolerance of the Church. Despite imprisonment in the Bastille, he continued to rail against the repression then rife in continental Europe.

## Adam Ferguson (1723–1816), Scottish social theorist

Ferguson argued that by pursuing their own happiness, people produced a world of creative diversity, of efficiency in the shape of division of labour, and of innovation, which drives progress. He explained the spontaneous nature of social institutions, writing: 'nations stumble upon establishments, which are indeed the result of human action, but not the execution of any human design'. These ideas informed his contemporary Adam Smith (1723–90).

## Adam Smith (1723–1790), Scottish philosopher and economist

Adam Smith mentions the 'invisible hand' only once in *The Wealth of Nations* (1776), but this powerful idea pervades the book. As his contemporary Adam Ferguson (1723–1816) had observed, human institutions may grow up without anyone intending them. Smith did not think people naturally selfish or disobliging, as they like others to think well of them; but they were self-interested, having a strong (but legitimate) interest in their own benefit. In the absence of coercion, they can realise that self-interest only by serving the interests of others; so in helping themselves, they help others too. Such voluntary exchange, Smith showed, creates value for *both* sides; they would not trade otherwise. He emphasised specialisation and the *division of labour*, made possible by the exchange process, as a major driver of efficiency and prosperity, both within and between nations: his influential arguments helped create the great nineteenth-century era of free trade. He was suspicious of crony capitalism and of big government. He felt that the 'man of system' (or social planner) could not possibly control the diverse motivations of humanity, and that the 'obvious and simple system of natural liberty' was a more enduring foundation for society.

## Thomas Jefferson (1743–1826), American revolutionary leader

Jefferson believed that God had given us all natural and 'unalienable' rights, including 'life, liberty and the pursuit of happiness'. He believed that people were naturally free to act as they pleased, provided that they did not infringe the similar freedom of others. Influenced by the ideas of John Locke (1632–1704), he maintained that the legitimacy of government rested on a contract between the people and their chosen representatives. He distrusted large concentrations of power, whether in government or business. He strongly opposed religious intolerance, as he did political absolutism.

## Frédéric Bastiat (1801–50), French political theorist

With trade restricted by Napoleon's 'Continental System', Bastiat argued for individual liberty and free markets. He regarded government as unreliable, inefficient and easily captured by producer interests, making it 'the great fiction through which everybody endeavours to live at the expense of everybody else'. He famously satirised protectionism with a spoof petition by candle makers, demanding government action against the competition they faced from the sun. Governments, he believed, existed to defend liberty and property – rights that predate them. Anticipating the Austrian School economists such as F. A. Hayek (1899–1992), he argued that markets, driven by self-interest, coordinated economic activity and steered resources to their most valued uses.

## Richard Cobden (1804–1865), English manufacturer and politician

With John Bright (1811–89), Cobden was leader of the Manchester School, which – following Adam Smith (1723–90) – maintained that free trade would make essential goods available to all and create a more equitable society. In 1838, they founded the Anti-Corn-Law League, urging (successfully) the abolition of protectionist tariffs against imported wheat, which raised bread prices and caused frequent shortages. They also campaigned for better understanding and peace between nations, which they believed free trade would promote. As a statesman, Cobden helped open up greater commerce between Britain and France.

## John Stuart Mill (1806–73), English philosopher and reformer

Mill's *On Liberty* (1859) is regarded as a classic libertarian text, though his defence of liberty is based on its beneficial results, not on abstract natural rights theory. Though a critic of big government, he nevertheless argued for state involvement on many fronts, not just its role in protecting freedom. Following his utilitarian mentor Jeremy Bentham (1748–1832), Mill thought that good was what produced the greatest happiness of the greatest number, though he also believed that higher pleasures outranked lower ones. Individuals should be free to follow their own desires, as long as they did not harm others in the process. The only legitimate use of government power was to prevent physical harm or the threat of it, and our mere disapproval of the actions of others, or their 'own good, physical and moral, is not sufficient warrant' to restrain them. Mill argued strongly for free speech, saying that silenced opinions might be correct, and even if wrong, provided a useful challenge to prevailing opinions.

## Herbert Spencer (1820–1903), English anthropologist and philosopher

Spencer sought to apply evolutionary theory to social and political affairs. He believed that human communities, originally simple and militaristic, had evolved into complex industrial societies, which spread because of their superior stability and prosperity. Despite being labelled a 'Social Darwinist', he thought that human beings were evolving into more benign creatures. He argued for the 'liberty of each, limited by the like liberty of all', and advocated small government, laissez faire and freedom of contract, opposing the regulation of trade and commerce.

He felt that freedom promoted diversity and innovation, which would enable societies to evolve more quickly and more beneficially.

## Friedrich A. Hayek (1899–1992), Anglo–Austrian political scientist

Hayek's economic works in the 1930s, researched with his mentor Ludwig von Mises, showed how boom and bust cycles arose from the inept government manipulation of credit; and he became the leading critic of collectivism, central planning and the expansionist interventionism of John Maynard Keynes (1883–1946), arguing that the latter would lead to inflation and economic dislocation. World War II led him to turn his attention to political science, and his best-selling *The Road to Serfdom* (1944) traced the roots of totalitarianism, arguing that central planning, being counterproductive, requires increasing compulsion to maintain. In *The Constitution of Liberty* (1960), he set out ideas for a free social and economic order. He updated the classical liberal idea of self-regulating, spontaneous social orders, showing how they emerge from the regular behaviour (or 'rules') followed by individuals. He argued that these orders, though unplanned, could process a huge amount of knowledge – held by individuals but dispersed, partial, personal and often ephemeral – more knowledge than any planning agency could process, even if it could access it. In *The Fatal Conceit* (1988), he argues that it is a delusion to imagine that we could shape such complex orders using the tools of the physical sciences, and that conscious attempts to redesign them would destabilise them and lead to social and economic disaster. Hayek also founded the Mont Pelerin Society, which has become a powerful international forum for classical liberal thinking.

## Ayn Rand (1905–82), Russian–American novelist and moralist

Expressed mainly through her novels, Rand championed a radical individualism, well on the libertarian end of the classical liberal spectrum. She saw life and self-actualisation as the moral standard. Reason, which underpinned that, should guide all our actions, and people should focus on their long-term, rational self-interest. Individuals were entitled to the fruits of their actions; nothing could be taken from them by force, which was abhorrent to the rational mind. But among rationally self-interested individuals there would in fact be no conflict, and no need for self-sacrifice, because people would see the value, to themselves, of respecting the rights of others. If there were a role for government, and for the rules of market activity, it was only to protect these rights.

## Isaiah Berlin (1909–97), Latvian–British philosopher

Berlin was the twentieth-century's leading philosophical defender of pluralism and toleration. No single model, he argued, could encapsulate the huge diversity and dynamism of human ideas, values and history. There was no single true moral principle, no fixed standard by which action could be judged: life was a constant compromise between different and often conflicting values, such as freedom and equality. He also distinguished two kinds of liberty. Negative liberty, exemplified in the work of John Stuart Mill (1806–73), upheld people's right to act without restraint. Positive liberty argued that people could not be free unless they could shape their own destiny and achieve self-actualisation. While there was merit in both concepts, Berlin feared that the positive freedom idea was being used by ideologues to undermine, not supplement, the negative freedom that remained the cornerstone of classical liberalism.

## Milton Friedman (1912–2006), American economist

In *Studies in the Quantity Theory of Money* (1956), Friedman revived the idea that government had a duty to keep the value of the currency stable. He argued that governments that tried to create employment by letting inflation rise would cause both inflation and unemployment. Inflation was like a drug, giving a short-term boost but bringing long-term problems. He therefore campaigned for a 'monetary rule' to prevent inflation, and for an end to deficit spending. With his wife Rose D. Friedman (1910–2009) he wrote the bestselling *Capitalism and Freedom* (1962), in which he argued for the then-radical ideas of free markets, floating exchange rates, a negative income tax, education vouchers and privatising state pensions. He believed that the only people to benefit from state regulation of professions were the professionals themselves, not their customers. He opposed criminalising drugs, saying that such lifestyle regulation undermined individual liberty. His book and TV series *Free to Choose* (1980) brought his arguments to an even wider audience. In it he wrote: 'Reliance on the freedom of people to control their own lives in accordance with their own values is the surest way to achieve the full potential of a great society'.

## James M. Buchanan (1919–2013), American economist

James Buchanan and Gordon Tullock (1922–2014) were the leading figures of the Public Choice School, co-authoring *The Calculus of Consent* (1962). They poured doubt on the rationality of democratic decisions, pointing out that the interests of particular voters, interest groups, politicians and officials all distort the process. While the 'welfare' economists pointed to *market failure*, the reality was that there was *government failure* too. Of particular concern was the ability of majorities – or even coalitions of small interest groups – to use the power of the state to exploit minorities, such as by levying taxes on particular groups of people. Buchanan believed that the best way to counter this was through a constitutional settlement that set the rules by which subsequent political decisions would be taken. Ideally, those constitutional rules should be decided unanimously so that nobody need leave themselves open, in subsequent decisions on law and regulation, to the tyranny of the majority.

## Robert Nozick (1938–2002), American philosopher

Nozick's *Anarchy, State, and Utopia* (1974) gave a thorough-going moral defence of liberty. It began with the 'categorical imperative' of Immanuel Kant (1724–1804), that we should treat others as ends in themselves, not as means to our ends; and therefore should act only in ways that we are prepared to make into a universal principle. Human beings, Nozick asserted, own their own bodies, talents and labour, which nobody has the right to take by force. Redistributive taxes are therefore unjustifiable. In any case, wealth did not exist to be shared out 'fairly'; it has to be created through the talent, entrepreneurship and effort of individuals. If wealth is acquired and transferred justly, without coercion, the resulting distribution of wealth among individuals must also be just, even though it will be unequal. The role of the state is solely to protect individuals against force, theft, fraud and breach of contract. But that leaves people free to pursue their own different goals and ambitions. Such a night-watchman state would not lead to anarchy – as many, after the French Revolution, had feared – because people would band together privately to protect their rights, for example, by creating private dispute resolution agencies.

# 11 CLASSICAL LIBERAL QUOTATIONS

## Magna Carta

We have also granted to all freemen of our kingdom, for us and our heirs forever, all the underwritten liberties, to be had and held by them and their heirs, of us and our heirs forever.... No scutage [tax] nor aid shall be imposed on our kingdom, unless by common counsel of our kingdom.... No freeman shall be taken or [and] imprisoned or disseised or exiled or in any way destroyed, nor will we go upon him nor send upon him, except by the lawful judgment of his peers or [and] by the law of the land.... To no one will we sell, to no one will we refuse or delay, right or justice. ... All merchants shall have safe and secure exit from England, and entry to England, with the right to tarry there and to move about as well by land as by water, for buying and selling by the ancient and right customs, quit from all evil tolls....

> – King John of England (1166–1216) (under duress)

## Natural rights

The right of nature ... is the liberty each man hath to use his own power, as he will himself, for the preservation of his own nature; that is to say, of his own life.

– Thomas Hobbes (1588–1679), *Leviathan*

The state of nature has a law of nature to govern it, which obliges every one: and reason, which is that law, teaches all mankind, who will but consult it, that being all equal and independent, no one ought to harm another in his life, health, liberty, or possessions....

– John Locke (1632–1704), *Two Treatises of Civil Government*

We hold these truths to be self-evident, that all men are created equal, that they are endowed by their Creator with certain inalienable rights, that among these are Life, Liberty, and the pursuit of Happiness.

– Thomas Jefferson (1743–1826),
*American Declaration of Independence*

Life, liberty and property do not exist because men have made laws. On the contrary, it was the fact that life, liberty and property existed beforehand that caused men to make laws in the first place.

– Frédéric Bastiat (1801–50), *The Law*

Individuals have rights and there are things no person or group may do to them (without violating their rights). So strong and far-reaching are these rights that they raise the question of what, if anything, the state and its officials may do.

– Robert Nozick (1938–2002), *Anarchy, State, and Utopia*

## Limited government

It is the highest impertinence and presumption ... in kings and ministers, to pretend to watch over the economy of private people, and to restrain their expense.... They are themselves always, and without any exception, the greatest spendthrifts in the society. Let them look well after their own expense, and they may safely trust private people with theirs. If their own extravagance does not ruin the state, that of their subjects never will.

– Adam Smith (1723–90), *The Wealth of Nations*

The powers of Government are of necessity placed in some hands; they who are intrusted with them have infinite temptations to abuse them, and will never cease abusing them, if they are not prevented.

– James Mill (1773–1836),'The State of the Nation',
in *The London Review*

Power tends to corrupt and absolute power corrupts absolutely.

– Lord Acton (1834–1902), *Letter to Bishop Creighton*

How can we keep the government we create from becoming a Frankenstein that will destroy the very freedom we establish it to protect? Freedom is a rare and delicate plant.... Government is necessary to preserve our freedom, it is an instrument through which we can exercise our freedom; yet by concentrating power in political hands, it is also a threat to freedom. Even though the men who wield this power initially be of good will ... the power will both attract and form men of a different stamp.

– Milton Friedman (1912–2006) with
Rose D. Friedman (1910–2009), *Capitalism and Freedom*

To the free man, the country is the collection of individuals who compose it, not something over and above them. He is proud of a common heritage and loyal to common traditions. But he regards government as a means, an instrumentality, neither a grantor of favors and gifts, nor a master or god to be blindly worshipped and served.

– Milton Friedman (1912–2006) with
Rose D. Friedman (1910–2009), *Capitalism and Freedom*

## Spontaneous order...

Every step and every movement of the multitude, even in what are termed enlightened ages, are made with equal blindness to the future; and nations stumble upon establishments, which are indeed the result of human action, but not the execution of any human design.

– Adam Ferguson (1723–1816),
*An Essay on the History of Civil Society*

[The rich] consume little more than the poor, and in spite of their natural selfishness and rapacity ... they divide with the poor the produce of all their improvements. They are led by an invisible hand to make nearly the same distribution of the necessaries of life, which would have been made, had the earth been divided into equal portions among all its inhabitants, and thus without intending it, without knowing it, advance the interest of the society, and afford means to the multiplication of the species.

– Adam Smith (1723–90), *The Theory of Moral Sentiments*

## ...Benign guidance...

Therefore a sage has said, 'I will do nothing (of purpose), and the people will be transformed of themselves; I will be fond of keeping still, and the people will of themselves become correct. I will take no trouble about it, and the people will of themselves become rich; I will manifest no ambition, and the people will of themselves attain to the primitive simplicity.'

– Lao Tzu (c. 600 BC)

Liberalism ... restricts deliberate control of the overall order of society to the enforcement of such general rules as are necessary for the formation of a spontaneous order, the details of which we cannot foresee.

– F. A. Hayek (1899–1992), *Rules and Order*

## …Versus planning and controls

The man of system … is apt to be very wise in his own conceit; and is often so enamoured with the supposed beauty of his own ideal plan of government, that he cannot suffer the smallest deviation from any part of it… He seems to imagine that he can arrange the different members of a great society with as much ease as the hand arranges the different pieces upon a chess-board. He does not consider that in the great chess-board of human society, every single piece has a principle of motion of its own, altogether different from that which the legislature might choose to impress upon it.

– Adam Smith (1723–90), *The Theory of Moral Sentiments*

[Without trade restrictions] the obvious and simple system of natural liberty establishes itself of its own accord. Every man … is left perfectly free to pursue his own interest in his own way…. The sovereign is completely discharged from a duty [for which] no human wisdom or knowledge could ever be sufficient; the duty of superintending the industry of private people, and of directing it towards the employments most suitable to the interest of the society.

– Adam Smith (1723–90), *The Wealth of Nations*

This is not a dispute about whether planning is to be done or not. It is a dispute as to whether planning is to be done centrally, by one authority for the whole economic system, or is to be divided among many individuals.

– F. A. Hayek (1899–1992), 'The Use of Knowledge in Society'

[B]efore we can try to remould society intelligently, we must understand its functioning; we must realize that, even when we believe that we understand it, we may be mistaken. What we must learn to understand is that human civilization has a life of its own, that all our efforts to improve things must operate within a working whole which we cannot entirely control, and the operation of whose forces we can hope merely to facilitate and assist so far as we can understand them.

– F. A. Hayek (1899–1992), *The Constitution of Liberty*

## Justice and the rule of law

That which is not just, is not Law; and that which is not Law, ought not to be obeyed.

– Algernon Sidney (1623–83),
*Discourses Concerning Government*

Where-ever law ends, tyranny begins, if the law be transgressed to another's harm; and whosoever in authority exceeds the power given him by the law, and makes use of the force he has under his command ... ceases in that to be a magistrate; and, acting without authority, may be opposed, as any other man, who by force invades the right of another.

– John Locke (1632–1704), *Two Treatises of Civil Government*

The political liberty of the subject is a tranquillity of mind arising from the opinion each person has of his safety....

When the legislative and executive powers are united in the same person, or in the same body of magistrates, there can be no liberty; because apprehensions may arise, lest the same monarch or senate should enact tyrannical laws, to execute them in a tyrannical manner.

– Montesquieu (1689–1755), *Spirit of the Laws*

Of great importance to the public is the preservation of this personal liberty; for if once it were left in the power of any the highest magistrate to imprison arbitrarily whomever he or his officers thought proper, (as in France it is daily practised by the crown,) there would soon be an end of all other rights and immunities.

– Sir William Blackstone (1723–80),
*Commentaries on the Laws of England*

If [justice] is removed, the great, the immense fabric of human society, that fabric which to raise and support seems in this world if I may say so has the peculiar and darling care of Nature, must in a moment crumble into atoms.

– Adam Smith (1723–90), *The Theory of Moral Sentiments*

A Spacious Hive well stockt with Bees,
That liv'd in Luxury and Ease....
They were not Slaves to Tyranny,
Nor rul'd by wild Democracy;
But Kings, that could not wrong, because
Their Power was circumscrib'd by Laws.

– Bernard Mandeville (1670–1733), *The Fable of the Bees*

## Economic freedom

Government means always coercion and compulsion and is by necessity the opposite of liberty. Government is a guarantor of liberty and is compatible with liberty only if its range is adequately restricted to the preservation of what is called economic freedom. Where there is no market economy, the best-intentioned provisions of constitutions and laws remain a dead letter.

– Ludwig von Mises (1881–1973), *Human Action*

To be controlled in our economic pursuits means to be ... controlled in everything.

– F. A. Hayek (1899–1992), *The Road to Serfdom*

Wherever we find any large element of individual freedom, some measure of progress in the material comforts at the disposal of ordinary citizens, and widespread hope of further progress in the future, there we also find that economic activity is organized mainly through the free market.

– Milton Friedman (1912–2006) and
Rose D. Friedman (1910–2009), *Free to Choose*

Few measures that we could take would do more to promote the cause of freedom at home and abroad than complete free trade.

– Milton Friedman (1912–2006) and
Rose D. Friedman (1910–2009), *Free to Choose*

## Personal freedom

No one has a right to compel me to be happy in the peculiar way in which he may think of the well-being of other men; but everyone is entitled to seek his own happiness in the way that seems to him best, if it does not infringe the liberty of others in striving after a similar end for themselves when their Liberty is capable of consisting with the Right of Liberty in all others according to possible universal laws.

– Immanuel Kant (1724–1804), *Principles of Politics*

They who can give up essential liberty to obtain a little temporary safety deserve neither liberty nor safety.

– Benjamin Franklin (1706–90),
*Reply to the Governor [of Pennsylvania]*

The only freedom which deserves the name is that of pursuing our own good, in our own way, so long as we do not attempt to deprive others of theirs, or impede their efforts to obtain it.

– John Stuart Mill (1806–73), *On Liberty*

The only purpose for which power can be rightfully exercised over any member of a civilised community, against his will, is to prevent harm to others. His own good, either physical or moral, is not sufficient warrant.

– John Stuart Mill (1806–73), *On Liberty*

Liberty lies in the hearts of men and women; when it dies there, no constitution, no law, no court can save it....

> – Judge Learned Hand (1872–1961),
> 'The Spirit of Liberty', 1944 New York speech

Our faith in freedom does not rest on the foreseeable results in particular circumstances but on the belief that it will, on balance, release more forces for the good than for the bad.

> – F. A. Hayek (1899–1992), *The Constitution of Liberty*

A society that puts equality before freedom will get neither. A society that puts freedom before equality will get a high degree of both.

> – Milton Friedman (1912–2006),
> *Free to Choose* (TV episode)

I'm in favor of legalizing drugs. According to my values system, if people want to kill themselves, they have every right to do so. Most of the harm that comes from drugs is because they are illegal.

> – Milton Friedman (1912–2006), quoted in
> *If Ignorance Is Bliss, Why Aren't There More Happy People?* by John Mitchinson

I wish the anarchists luck, since that's the way we ought to be moving now. But I believe we need government to enforce the rules of the game.... We need a government to maintain a system of courts that will uphold contracts and rule on compensation for damages. We need a government to ensure the safety of its citizens – to provide police protection. But government is failing at a lot of these things that it ought to be doing because it's involved in so many things it shouldn't be doing.

> – Milton Friedman (1912–2006), *Playboy* interview

## Political freedom

Political writers have established it as a maxim, that, in contriving any system of government, and fixing the several checks and controuls of the constitution, every man ought to be supposed a knave, and to have no other end, in all his actions, than private interest.

> – David Hume (1711–76), *Essays, Moral, Political, Literary*

Democracy and socialism have nothing in common but one word, equality. But notice the difference: while democracy seeks equality in liberty, socialism seeks equality in restraint and servitude.

> – Alexis de Tocqueville (1805–59),
> Speech to the Assembly, 1848

The state is the great fiction by which everyone seeks to live at the expense of everyone else.

> – Frédéric Bastiat (1801–50), *The State*

Democracy is essentially a means, a utilitarian device for safeguarding internal peace and individual freedom. As such it is by no means infallible or certain.

– F. A. Hayek (1899–1992), *The Road to Serfdom*

## 12  CLASSICAL LIBERALISM TIMELINE

930  The world's first Parliament, the Althing, founded in Iceland.

973  Anglo-Saxon King Edgar swears the first known coronation oath, pledging to defend the land, uphold the law, and rule justly.

1014  Anglo-Saxon King Aethelred agrees to uphold the ancient laws and be guided by the counsel of the Witan.

1066  Anglo-Saxon individual freedom and limited government is ended by the Norman invasion of England and the introduction of feudalism.

1215  Under pressure, King John agrees to Magna Carta, reasserting property rights and limiting the monarchy under the 'law of the land'.

1225  Henry III of England voluntarily reissues a new version of Magna Carta; it becomes a founding document of the British constitution.

1265  Simon de Montfort forms the Great Parliament, subjecting the king's decisions to approval by council, in consultation with Parliament.

1381  The Peasants' Revolt calls for England's ancient rights to be restored.

1517    Martin Luther sparks the Protestant Reformation, incidentally promoting greater individualism.

1651    Thomas Hobbes's *Leviathan* calls for strong government, but argues for a commonwealth built on social contract and for people's inalienable 'right of nature', to defend themselves, even against the state.

1687    William Penn publishes the first American printing of Magna Carta.

1688    In the Glorious Revolution, King James II is overthrown and Parliament lays out terms for the new sovereigns, William and Mary, setting out the limits of monarchical power.

1689    Great Britain's Bill of Rights stresses the contractual nature of government, lays down limits on the powers of the Crown, guarantees free speech in Parliament, stipulates regular elections and asserts the right to petition the authorities without fear of retribution.

1690    John Locke publishes his *Two Treatises on Civil Government*, providing philosophical foundations for the idea of contractual government and justifying the overthrow of King James II.

1705    Bernard Mandeville publishes *The Grumbling Hive*, a poem on the social benefits of self-interest.

1720    John Trenchard and Thomas Gordon start publishing *Cato's Letters*, newspaper essays promoting freedom of speech and conscience.

1734    Voltaire rails against the illiberal culture of France in *Philosophical Letters on the English*.

1748    Charles de Montesquieu publishes *The Spirit of the Laws*, urging the division of power into legislative, executive and judicial branches.

1767    Adam Ferguson's *History of Civil Society* describes how institutions can be 'the result of human action, but not the execution of any human design'.

1776    Thomas Paine's *Common Sense* accuses the British government of breaking its social contract with America, and incites revolution.

1776    Adam Smith publishes *The Wealth of Nations*, showing how self-interest, voluntary exchange, free trade and the division of labour all drive economic progress.

1776    America declares independence against the British government for violating the 'unalienable rights' of its citizens.

1780    John Adams's Constitution of Massachusetts enshrines the separation of powers, 'to the end it may be a government of laws, and not of men.'

1785    In *Groundwork for the Metaphysics of Morals*, Immanuel Kant outlines his 'categorical imperative' that other people should be treated as ends in themselves, not means to an end.

1789    The United States Constitution comes into force, encapsulating the division of power and limited government.

1789    France's revolutionary government publishes a *Declaration of the Rights of Man and of the Citizen*, asserting the no-harm rule, due process of law, property rights and freedom of conscience – but these principles are soon abandoned.

1791 The United States Bill of Rights is ratified, enumerating basic rights such as freedom of religion, speech, free assembly, a free press, the right to bear arms, and freedom from unjust arrest and seizure.

1833 Classical liberals' activism leads to the abolition of slavery throughout most of the British Empire.

1838 Richard Cobden and John Bright form the Anti-Corn-Law League aimed at abolishing harmful protectionist import tariffs on wheat.

1843 *The Economist*, founded by James Wilson, becomes a champion of free trade and laissez faire government.

1843 Slavery now abolished throughout the British Empire.

1846 The Corn Laws are abolished.

1849 Frédéric Bastiat's *The Law* asserts individuals' god-given right to defend their person, liberty and property, and argues that government and the law are illegitimate if they violate these rights.

1851 In *Social Statics*, Herbert Spencer makes an evolutionary case for a state limited to defending the persons and property of all individuals.

1859 John Stuart Mill publishes his classic defence of freedom, *On Liberty*.

1927 Ludwig von Mises reasserts classical liberal principles in *Liberalismus*, though it is not translated into English until 1962.

1943 Ayn Rand publishes her philosophical novel *The Fountainhead*, a powerful defence of self-fulfilment.

1944 F. A. Hayek publishes *The Road to Serfdom*, showing how the roots of totalitarianism lie in central planning and the coercion needed to back it up.

1945   In *The Open Society and Its Enemies*, Karl Popper makes the case against Utopian social engineering and outlines the idea of an 'open society', with diverse opinions and gradualist change.

1947   Classical liberal scholars from Europe and America congregate in Switzerland for the first meeting of the Mont Pelerin Society.

1957   Ayn Rand publishes the hugely influential *Atlas Shrugged*, asserting the critical importance of individual effort in creating prosperity.

1958   In *Two Concepts of Liberty*, Isaiah Berlin differentiates negative and positive liberty, saying that the latter is open to abuse by ideologues.

1960   F. A. Hayek publishes *The Constitution of Liberty*, outlining the roots, principles and institutions of a classical liberal society.

1962   *The Calculus of Consent* by James M. Buchanan and Gordon Tullock points out the problems of self-interest in political decision making.

1962   Milton Friedman publishes *Capitalism and Freedom*, which calls for free markets, floating exchange rates, a negative income tax, education vouchers and other ideas thought radical at the time.

1973   Murray Rothbard publishes *For a New Liberty*, a robust application of the natural rights tradition to modern social and political issues.

1974   Robert Nozick's *Anarchy, State, and Utopia*, a robust defence of freedom, opposes redistributive taxes as an assault on personal property.

1980  Milton Friedman's *Free to Choose* TV series brings classical liberal arguments to a new and wider audience.

1988  F. A. Hayek publishes *The Fatal Conceit*, explaining that the spontaneous order of human society is so complex that no individual planner could ever comprehend and direct it.

1989  The fall of the Berlin Wall reveals the economic backwardness and social problems of the centrally planned Soviet Bloc.

# 13 FURTHER READING

## Introductions

Ashford, N. (2013) *Principles for a Free Society*. Stockholm: Jarl Hjalmarson Foundation. Thorough, short exposition of the principles on which a free society and free economy are built.

Butler, E. (2011) *The Condensed Wealth of Nations*. London: Adam Smith Institute. Précis of Adam Smith's classical liberal economics, and of his ethics.

Butler, E. (2013) *Foundations of a Free Society*. London: Institute of Economic Affairs. Easy outline of the core principles underlying a free society, such as freedom, rights, toleration, the rule of law and limited government.

Friedman, M. with Friedman, R. D. (1962) *Capitalism and Freedom*. Chicago, IL: University of Chicago Press. Classic outline of the case for a free society and free economy, with radical policy prescriptions.

Friedman, M. and Friedman, R. D. (1980) *Free to Choose*. New York: Harcourt Brace Jovanovich. Engaging case for the free society, based on the television series of the same name.

Hannan, D. (2013) *How We Invented Freedom and Why It Matters*. London: Head of Zeus. Masterful tracing of classical liberal ideas from the Anglo-Saxon era to the present day.

Palmer, T. G. (2011) *The Morality of Capitalism*. Arlington, VA: Students for Liberty and Atlas Foundation. Short collection of essays on classical liberal morality, cooperation, progress, globalisation and culture.

Palmer, T. G. (ed.) (2013) *Why Liberty*. Arlington, VA: Students for Liberty and Atlas Foundation. Collection of essays on libertarian and classical liberal themes.

Palmer, T. G. (ed.) (2014) *Peace, Love, and Liberty*. Ottawa, IL: Jameson Books. Short but wide-ranging series of essays showing how social and economic freedom promotes international peace.

Pirie, M. (2008) *Freedom 101*. London: Adam Smith Institute. One hundred and one arguments against the free economy and free society, knocked down in a page each.

Wellings, R. (ed.) (2009) *A Beginner's Guide to Liberty*. London: Adam Smith Institute. Straightforward explanations of markets, property rights, liberty, government failure, prohibitions and welfare without the state.

## Overviews

Butler, E. (2011) *Milton Friedman: A Concise Guide to the Ideas and Influence of the Free-Market Economist*. Petersfield: Harriman House. Easy introduction to the economic and social ideas of the celebrated classical liberal economist.

Butler, E. (2012) *Friedrich Hayek: The Ideas and Influence of the Libertarian Economist*. Petersfield: Harriman House. Easy introduction to the classical liberal political scientist who developed much of the modern thinking on the spontaneous society.

Butler, E. (2012) *Public Choice – A Primer*. London: Institute of Economic Affairs. Simple explanation of government failure, the problems of self-interest in democratic systems, and the case for constitutional restraints.

Cranston, M. (1967) Liberalism. In *The Encyclopaedia of Philosophy* (ed. P. Edwards), pp. 458–461. New York: Macmillan and the Free Press.

Kukathas, C. (2003) *The Liberal Archipelago*. Oxford University Press. Powerful defence of diversity, multiculturalism and minority rights.

Meadowcroft, J. (ed.) (2008) *Prohibitions*. London: Institute of Economic Affairs. Powerful set of arguments against government controls on many different lifestyle choices.

Smith, G. H. (2013) *The System of Liberty: Themes in the History of Classical Liberalism*. Cambridge University Press. Outline of the history and different views of classical liberals on key issues such as order, justice, rights, anarchy and the role of the state.

## Classic texts

Bastiat, F. (2001) [1849] *Bastiat's 'The Law'*. London: Institute of Economic Affairs. Classic statement of classical liberal ideas from the French politician and writer.

Berlin, I. (1969) Two concepts of liberty. In *Four Essays on Liberty*. Oxford University Press. Article in which he distinguishes positive and negative liberty.

Hayek, F. A. (1944) *The Road to Serfdom*. London: Routledge. Classic short wartime exposition of the dangers of central planning and unrestrained government.

Hayek, F. A. (1960) *The Constitution of Liberty*. London: Routledge. Large book tracing the origins of liberal ideas and the principles on which a free society is founded.

Hayek, F. A. (1988) *The Fatal Conceit* (3 volumes). Chicago, IL: University of Chicago Press. Statement of the principles underpinning our spontaneous social and economic orders, and the case against trying to plan them centrally.

Hazlitt, H. (1946) *Economics in One Lesson*. New York, NY: Harper & Brothers. Still reckoned by many as the best introductory book on classical liberal economics.

Locke, J. (1960) [1689] *The Second Treatise of Government*. In *Two Treatises of Government* (ed. P. Laslett), pp. 283–446. Cambridge University Press. Philosophical justification of the idea of contractual and limited government, and of the right of the people to overthrow a government that breaches that contract.

Mill, J. S. (2008) [1859] On liberty. In *On Liberty and Other Essays* (ed. J. S. Mill). Oxford University Press. Classic text on the case for freedom, the no-harm principle, free speech, limited government, natural justice and toleration.

Popper, K. (1945) *The Open Society and Its Enemies*. London: Routledge. Philosophical defence of the free society and devastating critique of attempts to redesign society wholesale.

## Selected web links

Adam Smith Institute blog – rapidly changing blog of classical liberal viewpoints on current political, social and economic issues: http://www.adamsmith.org/blog/

Cato Institute – a leading Washington think tank committed to spreading the philosophy of liberty through research and media commentary: http://www.cato.org

IEA TV – short videos from the Institute of Economic Affairs on current issues, research, books, events and issues: http://www.iea.org.uk/tv

Learn Liberty – short videos from the Institute for Humane Studies, with classical liberal views on economics, politics, law, history and philosophy: http://www.learnliberty.org/videos/

Liberty League – promotes pro-freedom ideas among students and young professionals in the UK, and runs the UK's largest annual free-market conference: http://uklibertyleague.org

Mercatus Center – works to bridge the gap between academia and real world issues by training students, producing research, and producing solutions to social problems: http://mercatus.org

Online Library of Liberty – massive resource from the Liberty Fund, featuring key books and writings from classical liberals through the ages: http://oll.libertyfund.org

Reason Foundation – a leading US think tank that publishes a prominent magazine on market ideas and policy research: http://reason.org

Students for Liberty – a network of pro-freedom student groups, representing over 100,000 students in more than 1,350 groups worldwide: http://studentsforliberty.org

# ABOUT THE IEA

The Institute is a research and educational charity (No. CC 235 351), limited by guarantee. Its mission is to improve understanding of the fundamental institutions of a free society by analysing and expounding the role of markets in solving economic and social problems.

The IEA achieves its mission by:

- a high-quality publishing programme
- conferences, seminars, lectures and other events
- outreach to school and college students
- brokering media introductions and appearances

The IEA, which was established in 1955 by the late Sir Antony Fisher, is an educational charity, not a political organisation. It is independent of any political party or group and does not carry on activities intended to affect support for any political party or candidate in any election or referendum, or at any other time. It is financed by sales of publications, conference fees and voluntary donations.

In addition to its main series of publications the IEA also publishes a quarterly journal, *Economic Affairs*.

The IEA is aided in its work by a distinguished international Academic Advisory Council and an eminent panel of Honorary Fellows. Together with other academics, they review prospective IEA publications, their comments being passed on anonymously to authors. All IEA papers are therefore subject to the same rigorous independent refereeing process as used by leading academic journals.

IEA publications enjoy widespread classroom use and course adoptions in schools and universities. They are also sold throughout the world and often translated/reprinted.

Since 1974 the IEA has helped to create a worldwide network of 100 similar institutions in over 70 countries. They are all independent but share the IEA's mission.

Views expressed in the IEA's publications are those of the authors, not those of the Institute (which has no corporate view), its Managing Trustees, Academic Advisory Council members or senior staff.

Members of the Institute's Academic Advisory Council, Honorary Fellows, Trustees and Staff are listed on the following page.

The Institute gratefully acknowledges financial support for its publications programme and other work from a generous benefaction by the late Professor Ronald Coase.

The Institute of Economic Affairs
2 Lord North Street, Westminster, London SW1P 3LB
Tel: 020 7799 8900
Fax: 020 7799 2137
Email: iea@iea.org.uk
Internet: iea.org.uk

Other papers recently published by the IEA include:

*The Challenge of Immigration – A Radical Solution*
Gary S. Becker
Occasional Paper 145; ISBN 978-0-255-36613-7; £7.50

*Sharper Axes, Lower Taxes – Big Steps to a Smaller State*
Edited by Philip Booth
Hobart Paperback 38; ISBN 978-0-255-36648-9; £12.50

*Self-employment, Small Firms and Enterprise*
Peter Urwin
Research Monograph 66; ISBN 978-0-255-36610-6; £12.50

*Crises of Governments – The Ongoing Global Financial Crisis and Recession*
Robert Barro
Occasional Paper 146; ISBN 978-0-255-36657-1; £7.50

*… and the Pursuit of Happiness – Wellbeing and the Role of Government*
Edited by Philip Booth
Readings 64; ISBN 978-0-255-36656-4; £12.50

*Public Choice – A Primer*
Eamonn Butler
Occasional Paper 147; ISBN 978-0-255-36650-2; £10.00

*The Profit Motive in Education – Continuing the Revolution*
Edited by James B. Stanfield
Readings 65; ISBN 978-0-255-36646-5; £12.50

*Which Road Ahead – Government or Market?*
Oliver Knipping & Richard Wellings
Hobart Paper 171; ISBN 978-0-255-36619-9; £10.00

*The Future of the Commons – Beyond Market Failure and Government Regulation*
Elinor Ostrom et al.
Occasional Paper 148; ISBN 978-0-255-36653-3; £10.00

*Redefining the Poverty Debate – Why a War on Markets Is No Substitute for a War on Poverty*
Kristian Niemietz
Research Monograph 67; ISBN 978-0-255-36652-6; £12.50

*The Euro – the Beginning, the Middle … and the End?*
Edited by Philip Booth
Hobart Paperback 39; ISBN 978-0-255-36680-9; £12.50

*The Shadow Economy*
Friedrich Schneider & Colin C. Williams
Hobart Paper 172; ISBN 978-0-255-36674-8; £12.50

## Other IEA publications

Comprehensive information on other publications and the wider work of the IEA can be found at www.iea.org.uk. To order any publication please see below.

### Personal customers

Orders from personal customers should be directed to the IEA:

Clare Rusbridge
IEA
2 Lord North Street
FREEPOST LON10168
London SW1P 3YZ
Tel: 020 7799 8907. Fax: 020 7799 2137
Email: sales@iea.org.uk

### Trade customers

All orders from the book trade should be directed to the IEA's distributor:

NBN International (IEA Orders)
Orders Dept.
NBN International
10 Thornbury Road
Plymouth PL6 7PP
Tel: 01752 202301, Fax: 01752 202333
Email: orders@nbninternational.com

### IEA subscriptions

The IEA also offers a subscription service to its publications. For a single annual payment (currently £42.00 in the UK), subscribers receive every monograph the IEA publishes. For more information please contact:

Clare Rusbridge
Subscriptions
IEA
2 Lord North Street
FREEPOST LON10168
London SW1P 3YZ
Tel: 020 7799 8907, Fax: 020 7799 2137
Email: crusbridge@iea.org.uk